The
HOLY SPIRIT
in the
LATTER DAYS

The HOLY SPIRIT in the LATTER DAYS

by

Harold Lindsell

THOMAS NELSON PUBLISHERS
Nashville • Camden • New York

Published in Nashville, Tennessee, by Thomas Nelson, Inc. and distributed in Canada by Lawson Falle, Ltd., Cambridge, Ontario.

Printed in the United States of America.

Unless otherwise noted, all Scripture quotations are from The New King James Version. Copyright © 1979, 1980, 1982, Thomas Nelson, Inc., Publishers.

Scripture quotations noted RSV are from the Revised Standard Version of the Bible, copyrighted © 1946, 1952, 1971, 1973 by the Division of Christian Education of the National Council of the Churches of Christ in the U.S.A. and used by permission.

Scripture quotations noted NIV are from the Holy Bible: New International Version. Copyright © 1978 by the New York International Bible Society. Used by permission of Zondervan Bible Publishers.

Library of Congress Cataloging in Publication Data

Lindsell, Harold, 1913–
  The Holy Spirit in the latter days

  Bibliography: p. 203
  1. Holy Spirit.   2. Pentecostalism.   I. Title.
BT121.2.L56   1983   231'.3   83–3375
ISBN 0–8407–5279–2

Contents

PART I

The
TIMES
in which
WE LIVE

ONE

A Coming of Age

In a peculiar sense the latter half of the twentieth century may be said to be the coming of age of the Holy Spirit in the life of the church. Under the name "The Charismatic Movement" or "Neo-Pentecostalism," a new force swept over the Christian world in America and Latin America—even around the globe. Latin America, in particular, has experienced a mighty movement of God. This pentecostal phenomenon has been called by some observers the "Third Force" in the religious life and experience of that continent. The United States, too, has felt the impact of the charismatic awakening that has affected and influenced the Roman Catholic church and many, if not most, Protestant churches.

The phenomenon is both new and old. The current movement has roots that go back into church history for more than a century. Yet all of the components that make up the contemporary movement have been known and observed in the church in different places and at different times throughout the Christian world since Pentecost. But in the last century, the channeling together of a number of the components has introduced a new dimension in the religious life of the United States.

The Breadth of Interest

In recent decades the confluence of these diverse sources and traditions has affected all of American religious life. As a result, it may be said that in almost every Protestant denomination, as well as in the Roman Catholic church, the Holy Spirit for the first time is on "center stage" for numerous Christian people. By no means has the power of the Holy Spirit swept over great masses of people, and as yet we have seen no sweeping revival such as usually comes when the Spirit is greatly magnified. The present emphasis on the Holy Spirit has come at a moment in history when the secular, instead of the sacred, has become the prevailing factor in Western culture. Thus it is said we are living in the post-Christian era, for Europe has been thoroughly secularized. The United States, which has been moving more and more in the same direction, has not yet reached the advanced stage of spiritual apathy, decay, and decline found in Europe.

The modern ground swell of interest in the Holy Spirit may well be the best hope for a reversal of the secular trend in America. If this moment passes without any great awakening or substantial spiritual renewal among our people and churches, America may face the judgment of a righteous God who is giving us a last opportunity before He ravages the nation, dims the divine light, and allows the church in the West to become a church in the wilderness, hidden in certain nooks and crannies but unable to influence the course of history.

The churches in America, for the most part, suffer from a deep malaise. It is unlikely that they will be able to surmount their difficulties or rise up as towers of strength in a decadent culture. Most of the major denominations have been losing members steadily, and in the next twenty years their situation should be no better, since what membership they do have is growing older and will soon pass from the scene. They have not attracted and held the young people of the nation, for they frequently offer them little by way of a vital, dynamic faith. Nor do they impart to them a spirit of daring and self-sacrifice for evangelism and missionary outreach. A living church is a growing and expanding church. When the churches retreat, it is a sign of their decline. Even in the Roman Catholic church, a recent book entitled *The Fall and Decline of the Catholic Church* was written to point up that church's decline.

We must be clear that the humanist spirit abroad in the land has no connections with the Holy Spirit of God. It is man-centered and solely humane in its concern for the material state of the oppressed and the poor. It arrogantly asserts that the economically productive people are *de facto* the enemies of mankind and the source of the world's ills.

As far back as 1924, one prescient professor at Harvard University published a book, *Democracy and Leadership,* in which he forecast the present debacle. He said,

> With the present trend toward "social justice," the time is rapidly approaching when everybody will be minding everybody else's business. For the conscience that is felt as a still small voice and that is the basis of real justice, we have substituted a social conscience that operates rather through a megaphone. The busybody, for the first time perhaps in the history of the world, has been taken at his own estimate of himself.

Professor Babbitt went on to argue that a democratic people, lacking in moral discipline, will soon fall prey to a ruthless totalitarianism. Only the Holy Spirit can provide the moral discipline a nation needs, and that will not eventuate until its people place themselves under the sovereignty of the Spirit and walk, by His power, in obedience to the divine commandments.

The Converging Streams

In the United States, the Mississippi is the largest river, into which many other rivers flow. For example, the Wabash River flows into the Ohio River, and the waters from both flow into the Mississippi. The Missouri River also flows into the Mississippi, as do the Illinois and the Arkansas rivers. Similarly, we may say that the present-day charismatic phenomenon is a combination of tributary movements flowing into and making up the larger contemporary movement. Let us make a brief and highlighted survey of some of these streams.

The Holiness Movement

The first of the converging streams that make up the present charismatic phenomenon is the holiness movement. This had its modern beginnings in the revival in England in the eighteenth century. Lecky, the English historian, noted that this spiritual awakening not only altered the face of England but also saved it from the same sort of revolution that overtook France shortly thereafter and led to the atheistic secularization of that nation. The English awakening was sparked by John and Charles Wesley and George Whitefield. The Wesleys were Arminians; Whitefield was a Calvinist. But all were evangelists, and all stressed the life of holiness, albeit from different perspectives and with varying emphases. The modern holiness movement, of which we speak here, owes its greatest debt, however, to John Wesley.

John Wesley, the founding genius of Methodism and the holiness movement, experienced a cataclysmic spiritual awakening at Aldersgate. From that moment onward he was a transformed man. While there is no record that he ever spoke in tongues, he was certainly filled with the Holy Spirit and evidenced many other spiritual gifts.

The holiness movement has always associated the life of power in the Spirit alongside the life of holiness. The Holy Spirit endowed John Wesley with the gift of an evangelist and supplied him with the mighty power that enabled him to preach the gospel with astounding success. He saw great numbers of conversions as he traversed England from one end to the other. The Methodist church emerged from Wesley's labors, was transplanted to the American colonies, and became the largest Protestant body, until it was recently surpassed by the Southern Baptist Convention. For many years the Methodist churches, north and south, were probably the most potent evangelistic agencies in American life.

One of the major contributions of John Wesley was his personal commitment to a life of holiness. The resultant holiness doctrine emphasized sinless perfection or "eradication." While there might have been differences concerning perfectionism among the holiness people, one perception stood out starkly. They all believed that entire sanctification was a work of grace that came to believers after conversion and before physical death. The stressing of holiness was always accompanied by revivalistic evangelism and missionary outreach. In its theology, the holiness movement generally embraced the Arminian tradition.

The English Wesleyan awakening spread to colonial America at the time when the colonies became a nation and the westward expansion began. Methodist circuit riders followed the advancing frontiers, along with the Baptists. The old saw is that the Methodists and the Baptists came on foot and horseback; the Presbyterians waited for the railroad; the Episcopalians waited for the Pullman cars.

Wherever Methodism took root, the holiness doctrine was proclaimed. But once Methodism had established itself deeply in American culture, and as the pulpit and the pew became better educated and experienced upward social mobility, the emphasis on entire sanctification lessened. Throughout the nineteenth century, however, the Wesleyan holiness movement was quite strong. Along with the establishment of the major Methodist denominations in the north and south, smaller holiness groups sprouted up all over America and around the world.

The largest present-day non-Methodist holiness denomination in the United States is the Church of the Nazarene, which has its headquarters in Kansas City, Missouri. It sprang from the merger of some fifteen religious bodies that were part of the American holiness movement. The first merger took place in 1907, when the Church of the Nazarene united with the Association of Pentecostal Churches of America to form the Pentecostal Church of the Nazarene. Other groups joined the newly founded denomination. In 1919 the term *pentecostal* was dropped from the denominational name. This action was taken because the word *pentecostal* was increasingly associated with speaking in tongues, which was not high on the agenda for the Nazarenes. They did emphasize a second work of grace, or entire sanctification, but dropped some of the other emphases characteristic of pentecostals.

There are a number of smaller holiness bodies in America today. In 1867 the Christian Holiness Association, which is still in existence, was organized. According to its literature, it is "a coordination agency of those religious bodies that hold the Wesleyan-Arminian theological view." Its central office is in Indianapolis, Indiana, and it is made up of affiliated and cooperating organizations. The affiliated organizations include the Brethren in Christ Church, the Churches of Christ in Christian Union, the Evangelical Church of North America, the Evangelical Friends Alliance, the Evangelical Methodist Church, the Free Methodist Church of North America, the Holiness Christian Church of the U.S.A., The Canadian Holiness Federation, The Church of the Nazarene, The Salvation Army, The Salvation Army in Canada, and the Wesleyan Church. The cooperating organizations include the Methodist Protestant Church, the Primitive Methodist Church, The Congregational Methodist Church, The Church of God (Anderson), The Missionary Church, and The Sanctified Church of Christ. Today the United Methodist Church, the second largest Protestant body in America, is not related to this association.

One of the distinctive badges of the smaller holiness bodies is their emphasis on entire sanctification. Moreover, there are small groups within the United Methodist Church for whom the holiness teaching is still promoted. The holiness sector of America's holiness movement also has in its orbit a number of Bible schools, colleges, and theological seminaries. Among the independent institutions are Asbury College and Asbury Theological Seminary. These institutions are distinctively Methodist. While they are not owned and controlled by the United Methodist Church, they serve it through their graduates as they do the affiliated and cooperating churches of the Christian Holiness Association.

The modern charismatic movement is indebted to those who constitute the holiness tradition today, even though some in the holiness movement are not actively associated with the charismatic phenomenon. The groups in which the holiness perspective was dominant, and evangelistic zeal and missionary outreach were promoted, have had a strong influence among the burgeoning group of believers who are deeply interested in, and concerned with, the work of the Holy Spirit. The life of holiness and the work of the Holy Spirit are so interrelated that the one cannot be found without the other.

The Pentecostal Movement

The pentecostal churches constitute a second contributary stream that has influenced the emergence of the charismatic movement. The spark that ignited the modern pentecostal flame was lit on New Year's Day of 1901. The site was Topeka, Kansas, where Charles Parham's Bible School was located. A New Year's Eve service continued on into New Year's Day. Charles Parham laid hands on one of the students, Agnes Ozman, who was then baptized in the Spirit. She began to speak in a strange tongue. Her experience was followed by the same manifestation among other students in the school. Similar works of the Spirit in the gift of tongues were then noted here and there around America. But it was sporadic at first.

In 1906 the newly emergent pentecostal phenomenon was given impetus in the city of Los Angeles. Some white and black people gathered in a private home for a sort of pre-Pentecost prayer meeting. On April 9 a black lad spoke in tongues. Six others likewise spoke in tongues shortly thereafter. The crowds increased, and the group moved into an abandoned Baptist church on Azusa Street, in a new commercial area where there was a stable and a lumber yard. A black preacher, W. S. Seymour, led the services. He was uneducated, blind in one eye, and by no means an outstanding preacher. In fact, he did not preach very much. But in the space of three years, thousands of people received the baptism of the Spirit. They had flocked to Los Angeles from all over America and around the world.

Out of these small beginnings churches were founded, denominations came into being, and the modern pentecostal movement was well on its way. In October of 1948, the Pentecostal Fellowship of North America (PFNA) was organized at Des Moines, Iowa. This came shortly after the first World Conference of Pentecostal Believers was held in Zurich, Switzerland, in May of 1947. The PFNA has for its objectives, according to the *Yearbook of Churches,*

> (1) to provide a vehicle of expression and coordination of efforts in matters common to all member bodies including missionary and evangelistic effort; (2) to demonstrate to the world the essential unity of Spirit-baptized believers; (3) to provide services to its constituents to facilitate world evangelism; (4) to encourage the principles of comity for the nurture of the body of Christ, endeavoring to keep the unity of the Spirit until we all come to the unity of the faith.

The PFNA has local chapters in communities where churches of the member groups are located, and fellowship rallies are held. On the national level, representatives of the member bodies are assembled for studies and exchange of views in the fields of home missions, foreign missions and youth.

The members of the PFNA include the following: the Anchor Bay Evangelistic Association, the Assemblies of God, the Carolina Evangelistic Association, the Christian Church of North America, the Church of God of Apostolic Faith, the Church of God (Cleveland, Tenn.), the Church of God, Mountain Assembly, the Congregational Holiness Church, Elim Fellowship, the Emmanuel Holiness Church, the Free Gospel Church, Inc., the Free Will Baptist (Pentecostal Faith), the International Church of the Foursquare Gospel, the International Pentecostal Assemblies, the Italian Pentecostal Church of Canada, the Open Bible Standard Churches, Inc., the Pentecostal Assemblies of Canada, the Pentecostal Assemblies of Newfoundland, the Pentecostal Church of God of America, the Pentecostal Church of Christ, the Pentecostal Free-Will Baptist, the Pentecostal Holiness Church, and the Pentecostal Holiness Church of Canada.

Three of the pentecostal churches together number approximately two million people (the Assemblies of God, the Church of God [Cleveland, Tenn.], and the United Pentecostal Church). This indicates the strength of the pentecostal work, which is significant, if for no other reason than because it is a twentieth century movement quite unlike the major denominations whose traditions go back to the Reformation of the sixteenth century.

Pentecostal churches through the years have manifested an enthusiasm that, at times, has led to abuse, or at least to unusual happenings, foreign to the more staid mainline churches. The services have included such biblically recorded activities as speaking in tongues, interpretation of tongues, miracles of healing, discernment of spirits, as well as dancing in the aisles, "slaying in the spirit," and other enthusiasms, sometimes of a loud sort.

Central to the pentecostal tradition, then and now, is speaking in other tongues. This manifestation has brought criticism from a variety of sources. Some in the dispensational tradition think speaking in tongues has not been valid since the end of the first century. For that reason, tongues has been looked upon by some as demonic or, at best, counterfeit.

According to the pentecostal tradition, tongues enables a believer to pray in a language he or she has never learned, as described in the Book of Acts. The speaker generally does not understand what he or she is saying, nor in most instances today does the listener know the tongue that is spoken.

When such a phenomenon occurs, of course, it is open to possible abuse. Some who exercise the gift think they have been given a new revelation. In some cases, excesses, wrong opinions, and unbiblical elements creep in. The stress on an inner light leads some who manifest such an experience to suppose they are above the church and its authority. Occasionally pride drives some to claim and exercise authority to which they have no right.

When all of this has been said, and all of the less desirable elements have been catalogued, however, there remains a solid core of biblically sound pentecostal believers who possess something that people from other traditions know nothing about. It is virtually impossible to sustain the view that there can be no manifestation of tongues today. At the same time, it can be said that some of the favorable statements about tongues may claim more than the biblical evidences allow.

Like those in the holiness movement, pentecostals believe there is a work of grace that is available to all believers subsequent to the new birth. It is something every Christian should seek and can attain. The pentecostal tradition differs from the holiness camp in that the blessing of God has for its sign of fulfillment the gift of tongues. In other words, if the recipient does not speak in tongues, then the blessing has not come. The pentecostals call this experience the baptism in the Spirit. We will show later that the baptism in the Spirit is related to a life of holiness. In that sense, the pentecostals share something in common with the holiness people.

By making the gift of tongues an essential element of their theology, the pentecostal denominations have introduced a dividing doctrine that is unacceptable to those who reject the notion that tongues is an indispensable ingredient of an orthodox theology. The doctrine of tongues also supposes, by reason of its significance for pentecostals, that those who do not receive the gift are, in effect, living an inferior Christian life; they are defective believers.

On the other hand, holding to the doctrine of tongues has not prevented a denomination like the Assemblies of God from becoming a member of the National Association of Evangelicals (NAE), which says nothing in its doctrinal platform about the gift or use of tongues. The pentecostals in the National Association of Evangelicals have worked well in this cooperative body. The current head of the Assemblies of God, Thomas Zimmerman, has served as one of the presidents of the NAE. He was on the central committee of the Congress for World Evangelization that was held in Lausanne, Switzerland, and was chairman of the American Festival of Evangelism, which met in Kansas City, Missouri, in the summer of 1981.

No one can overlook the fact that "glossolalia," or speaking in tongues, and its highly important role in the structures of the pentecostal churches has been a tension point for the churches, institutions, and parachurch organizations that have reservations about speaking in tongues. Some oppose tongues as the sign of the baptism in the Spirit, as well as the term "baptism in the Spirit" itself. Those of this perception usually deny tongues speaking of any sort for any reason. Others, who do not accept tongues as *the* or even *a* sign of the baptism, do acknowledge the legitimacy of tongues as one of the gifts of the Spirit, given only to those to whom the Spirit wishes to give the gift. Later we will address the question whether the terms "the baptism in (or *of*) the Spirit" and being "filled with the Spirit" are generically different terms, or whether they represent the same biblical truth under two different names.

Other Contributions to the Charismatic Movement

This brings us to the third stream of influence that has gone into the formation of the charismatic movement as it is known and promoted in our day. This third component is not as easily characterized, and it is certainly more resistant to definition because of its disparate nature. It is difficult to give a particular name to this manifestation that would adequately cover the waterfront it represents.

In this past century, apart from the holiness and the pentecostal movements, other less identifiable and less organized strands of comparable influence surfaced and helped to promote the charismatic phenomenon we see today. In these instances, it is fair to say that the originators of some of these emphases could not have foreseen to what they would lead in the future. And they would have been among the first to warn against some of the current fads. Let me note several of the more prominent leaders.

Dwight Lyman Moody and R. A. Torrey represent, in the field of evangelism, a strong team who elaborated on their conviction that effective evangelism requires, on the part of the evangelists, an experience they called the "baptism with the Spirit." It should be noted that Moody, who founded what became the Moody Bible Institute, was forever urging R. A. Torrey to speak on the subject of the baptism with the Spirit. It was an experience that both of them shared and that they promoted with passionate interest. R. A. Torrey headed up the Moody Bible Institute in Chicago for a time, and later he was one of the founding fathers of the Bible Institute of Los Angeles (Biola University).

Today, neither the Moody Bible University nor Biola University identify themselves with the phrase used by both Moody and Torrey—the baptism with the Spirit. It may be, of course, that the term had different connotations for Moody and Torrey than it does today. Or they may have been speaking about something that the Moody Bible Institute and Biola University would endorse with enthusiasm, that is, being filled with the Spirit. In any event, the experiences of both Moody and Torrey, their statements about those experiences, and the books of R. A. Torrey must be considered an important contribution to the developing charismatic movement of our day. Neither Moody nor Torrey, however, placed any importance on speaking in tongues in connection with the baptism with the Spirit.

A. B. Simpson and the Christian and Missionary Alliance (CMA), which he founded, also stressed certain doctrines commonly manifested in the charismatic movement. Simpson and the CMA have constantly believed in divine healing. Numbers of people were healed under the ministry of A. B. Simpson, and some of the present leaders of the CMA have experienced personal healings. Dr. Simpson also strongly endorsed the biblical teaching about the Spirit-filled life. He wrote a two-volume work on the Holy Spirit that enjoyed a large circulation. The Alliance is widely known today for its splendid missionary outreach. Indeed, no other small denomination supports more missionaries overseas for its size than does the Alliance. But missionary passion is not one of the outstanding characteristics of the charismatic movement in America.

Andrew Murray of South Africa also contributed greatly to

the modern charismatic phenomenon through his books on holiness. He has been, and still is, one of the most widely read writers on this subject. Holiness, of course, is inseparable from the person and work of the Holy Spirit. The Spirit-filled life, or the life of victory, was one of Murray's great gifts to American evangelicalism.

The same is true for the Keswick movement in England, which was transplanted to America and then thrived under the leadership of men like Robert McQuilkin of the Columbia Bible College in South Carolina. The Spirit-filled life, with its stress on holy living, received a great boost from the Keswick movement and from those in America who supported it enthusiastically. One of the greatest spiritual awakenings ever to come to Wheaton College occurred in 1936 when Robert McQuilkin was the speaker. The consequences flowing out of that one taste of the Spirit's power were felt around the world. Hundreds of lives were touched and blessed. The effects of that awakening continue today, and this has been testified to by those who were students at the college when it happened. Similar manifestations of the Spirit's power have overtaken other schools, such as Asbury College and Houghton College.

A. J. Gordon, through his pulpit, books, and educational labors, influenced Unitarian New England and the entire United States. He founded what was later to become Gordon College and Divinity School, which in turn led to the merger of Gordon Divinity School and Conwell School of Theology as a separate entity from Gordon College. A. J. Gordon's books on the Spirit-filled life have had a continuing ministry in their own right.

Men like these—Moody, Torrey, Simpson, Murray, Gordon—have all had a lasting impact on today's charismatics, both through their writings and the institutions they founded. Check, for example, the bibliographies in the books of modern charismatic authors. You may be surprised at how often these older authors are used as both theological and inspirational source material. And the next time you pay a visit to Wheaton College, or Gordon, or Asbury, ask the students you meet how they came to Christ. You will discover many were reached through the charismatic movement. As for the theology they are learning, much of it is the same as that believed by these same men one hundred years ago.

The Rise of the Charismatic Movement

Springing from the antecedents that we have described briefly, the modern charismatic movement has come to the fore. The past two decades have witnessed a phenomenon that is ecumenical in its orientation, spiritual in its emphasis, and widespread in its outreach. It has touched virtually every mainline denomination—liberal and conservative—the Roman Catholic church, and multitudes of individuals everywhere. Episcopalians, Methodists, Lutherans, Presbyterians, Baptists, and hordes of Christians from every walk of life in and out of the churches of America have found help, by which they have been enabled to live on a higher spiritual plane.

The movement has been inclusive enough to embrace tongues and healing. It has transcended even important theological differences. It has brought together for mass meetings people who would never have joined hands or hearts before. Its outreach has been aided by radio and television. In the latter case, the 700 Club, with its extensive television coverage and its programming under the aegis of Pat Robertson, has dramatized what is happening in so many instances.

The pattern of the movement is variegated. There is no central clearing house and no formal organization. Traces of the movement's influence can be seen in hundreds of weekly Bible classes that meet in private homes. It attracts thousands of people who attend small meetings around the country almost every night of the week. The person and work of the Holy Spirit in the lives of people today lie at the heart of the movement.

The United Presbyterian Church (UPCUSA, northern) appointed a committee to look into this phenomenon. At the 182nd General Assembly in 1970, that church received the *Report of the Special Committee on the Work of the Holy Spirit*. In the report it was stated that glossolalia is not pathological, nor hysterical, nor schizophrenic. The committee advocated "a position of 'openness' regarding the Neo-Pentecostal movement within our denomination." It said that "the advent of Neo-Pentecostalism into our denomination may be one aspect of reformation and renewal." In 1971 the Presbyterian Church in the United States (PCUS, southern) heard a similar report. In 1975 the Baptist General Conference received a report that advocated a sober but open and positive stance in regard to the gifts of the Spirit.

A number of ecclesiastical leaders of the Roman Catholic church have also shown enthusiasm for the movement. One energetic advocate of talks with Rome, David DuPlessis, who has pentecostal roots, has sponsored dialogue with the Roman Catholic church at the highest levels. Mr. DuPlessis' striking forte is his insistence on tongues speaking as *the* sign of the baptism.

General Observations

It must be said that the absence of a definitive biblical and historical theology in other areas than that of the person and work of the Holy Spirit is one of the drawbacks of the current charismatic movement. It is very difficult, for example, to see how evangelicals and Roman Catholics can unite around the presence and power of the Spirit without talking about the major points of disagreement in essential areas of theology. It must be recognized, however belatedly, that numbers of Roman Catholics have been personally converted to Christ and are surely sons and daughters of God. In many cases, they have put "on hold" the important doctrinal areas where evangelicals and the Roman Catholic church differ. Multitudes remain in the church, believing they have a missionary ministry to bring the full gospel to other Roman Catholics. But it is not appropriate for evangelicals to give anyone the impression that the differences between their views and the official teachings of the Roman Catholic church are unimportant or that they do not represent continuing stumbling blocks to fellowship.

In addition, the entire subject of speaking in tongues and its relationship to the filling of the Holy Spirit continues to be a thorny question beset with all kinds of difficulties. In this connection, the terminology employed by some charismatics and pentecostals when they speak of the Holy Spirit's power, namely "the baptism in, with, or of the Holy Spirit" represents an implied threat and is a source of concern to many evangelicals. Whether these are theological problems, problems of nomenclature, or simply psychological hangovers from earlier days that should no longer hinder the most intimate fellowship is another matter. We will look at all of this later.

Surely our age has produced anxieties and frustrations, and has surfaced deep spiritual needs, for which many Christians are seeking answers. The loss of deep conviction in the area of theology, occasioned by the rise of the Enlightenment and the loss of faith in the basic distinctives of the Christian faith, troubles many believers. These Christian people are looking for certainties. They want something they can hang on to, both in life and at death. They welcome the truth that God is still at work in this torn world, in the person of the Holy Spirit. They rejoice that the Spirit of God dwells in their hearts and that He witnesses to the truth of their Christian convictions. They also know they have a need for power in their lives if they are to walk and work with the joy of the Lord in them. The Holy Spirit is their best, and surely their brightest, hope. If this is not so, to whom can they turn, and what is there to provide that for which their hearts yearn?

It is with these challenges in mind that we begin our journey in the Scriptures, taking a fresh look at Pentecost, as well as seeking to discover what happened before and after Pentecost and throughout the latter days in the lives of the people of God. (By the "latter days," we refer to that expanse of time inaugurated at Pentecost and stretching forth to those days immediately preceding the Second Coming of Jesus Christ.) We do so with the understanding that the basic theology underlying the search is nothing less than that which is commonly called historic orthodoxy. We are committed to this theological system, and in the light of that, we will pursue our study of the person and the work of the Holy Spirit in those areas where the tensions exist.

We start by acknowledging the truth that the Holy Spirit is the third person of the blessed Trinity. He possesses all of the divine attributes common to the Father and the Son. He was sent by the Father and the Son and is worshiped together with the Father and the Son, so that we now live in what might well be called the Age of the Holy Spirit. He is our teacher, and we look with faith for Him to open the eyes of our understanding and to guide us into the fullness of divine truth.

PART II

The
BIBLICAL FAITH
and the
HOLY SPIRIT

Two

The Holy Spirit,
the Patriarchs, and the Kings

The Godhead exists eternally in three persons: the Father, the Son and the Holy Spirit. Yet Christians are not tritheists. They are monotheists, insisting that God is one in essence or nature, while maintaining that there are three persons, or a trinity of persons, fully sharing that one nature according to the revelation of Scripture. The Godhead is, thus, one in three, three in one.

The Word of God states that each member of the Trinity performs functions that belong exclusively to each one, and these offices are nontransferable. It was the Son who died on the cross of Calvary, not the Father or the Holy Spirit. It was the Father who sent the Son to die for the salvation of mankind. The Holy Spirit is the third person of the Trinity, whose special work in the church began at Pentecost. He was sent by the Father and the Son. Christ, in His glorified human body, sits at the right hand of the Father in heaven and is the omnipresent head of the church in the person of the Holy Spirit who indwells every believer.

Some believers suppose that the age before Jesus Christ was the age of the Father. Then came the age of the Son, when He became incarnate and dwelt in the flesh on earth. Now we live in the age of the Holy Spirit. This is partially true in that, functionally, the work of each member of the Trinity dominated the historical scene while performing His particular work. But this does not mean that when the Son of God was on earth the Father and the Holy Spirit were inactive. The Godhead, comprising the three persons, has been at work at all times in the history of redemption.

Thus, when we think about the special work of the Holy Spirit in the latter days, we must not suppose that the Holy Spirit was not at work in Old Testament times. For any serious study of the Old Testament will disclose that the Holy Spirit was mightily present during that age. There were differences in what He did at that time from what He is doing today. At the same time, there were similarities with the work He is doing today. What the similarities and differences are, we need to discover and understand. It is far easier to comprehend the working of the Holy Spirit following Pentecost when we have observed how He worked in the Old Testament period. And His work in our midst, in our day, is far better understood as we study His ministry before Pentecost.

First we should speak of the work of the Holy Spirit in the area of His general operations, and then of His work in the lives of specific individuals. From this study we will see how extensive the activities of the Spirit were and how important they are in the story of redemption. Oftentimes an apparently incidental mention of a work of the Holy Spirit opens up vistas of considerable importance. These instances need to be studied and the implications of the numerous works of the Spirit made plain to us.

The General Works of the Holy Spirit

The Holy Spirit was deeply involved in the original creation. Genesis 1:1 reads, "In the beginning God created the heavens and the earth." Then it is revealed that "the Spirit of God was hovering over the face of the waters" (v. 2). Yes, the Holy Spirit was active in the creation of all things. It was the work of the Trinity: the Father, the Son, and the Holy Spirit.

The Holy Spirit is spoken of as the author of life. Elihu, in his speech to Job, said, "But there is a spirit in man, and the breath of the Almighty gives him understanding," and "For I am full of words; The spirit within me compels me" (Job 32:8,18). Then Elihu proclaimed the great truth of his origins: "The Spirit of God has made me,/And the breath of the Almighty gives me life" (Job 33:4). Moreover, the Lord Jesus Christ was conceived by the Holy Spirit. It was He who so mysteriously came on the Virgin Mary and impregnated her with God the Son: "The Holy Spirit will come upon you, and the power of the Most High will overshadow you. So the holy one to be born will be called the Son of God" (Luke 1:35 NIV).

The Holy Spirit is the divine author of the written Word of God. This is stated in the New Testament by Peter, who said, "For prophecy never came by the will of man, but holy men of God spoke as they were moved by the Holy Spirit" (2 Pet. 1:21).

The evidences for this special work of the Spirit in the Old Testament are overwhelming. Nehemiah wrote,

> "Yet for many years You had patience with them,
> And testified against them by Your Spirit in Your prophets.
> Yet they would not listen;
> Therefore You gave them into the hand of the peoples of the
>   lands" (Neh. 9:30).

Isaiah recorded this word from God: "'As for Me,' says the LORD, 'this is My covenant with them: My Spirit who is upon you, and My words which I have put in your mouth, shall not depart from your mouth, nor from the mouth of your descendants, nor from the mouth of your descendants' descendants,' says the LORD, 'from this time and forevermore'" (Is. 59:21). We are also told, "Then the Spirit came upon Amasai, chief of the captains, and he said:

'We are yours, O David;
We are on your side, O son of Jesse!
Peace, peace to you,
And peace to your helpers!
For your God helps you'" (1 Chr. 12:18).

The New Testament also bears witness to the Old Testament's statement by David in Psalm 110. Jesus Himself was speaking to the Pharisees: "He said to them, 'How then does David in the Spirit call Him "Lord," saying:

"The LORD said to my Lord,
'Sit at My right hand,
Till I make Your enemies
    Your footstool'"? (Matt. 22:43–44).

David's words were the Spirit's words and the Spirit's words were the Word of God written, which we have today.

The general working of the Holy Spirit in Israel is stated categorically by Isaiah:

But they [Israel] rebelled and grieved His Holy Spirit;
So he turned Himself against them as an enemy,
And He fought against them.
Then he remembered the days of old,
Moses and his people, saying:
"Where is He who brought them up out of the sea
With the shepherd of His flock?
Where is He who put His Holy Spirit within them,
Who led them by the right hand of Moses,
With His glorious arm,
Dividing the water before them . . . ?" (Is. 63:10–12).

Indeed, the Spirit is said to have been at work in the midst of Israel. The Holy Spirit was "set among them." When they rebelled, they are said to have grieved the Holy Spirit. This

34

could not have been true had not the Holy Spirit been present and at work in their midst. They rejected His presence, His works, and His words, and He was grieved, even as Christians in their context today can grieve the Holy Spirit. Since revelation is progressive, and the New Testament tells us more about the present work of the Holy Spirit, this does not mean we should undervalue or pay less attention to His work in the Old Testament period.

In John 16:8, Jesus said that when the Holy Spirit "has come, He will convict the world of sin, and of righteousness, and of judgment." Did He mean by this that the Holy Spirit was to perform a new work, a work He did not perform in the Old Testament period? Indeed not. Genesis 6:3 says, "And the LORD said, 'My Spirit shall not strive with man forever, for he is indeed flesh; yet his days shall be one hundred and twenty years.'" This text makes it plain that the Holy Spirit was at work in the hearts of men in the Old Testament; He was bringing conviction of sin, righteousness, and judgment from the very start.

The Old Testament also speaks of the omnipresence of the Holy Spirit in relation to the people of God. In Psalm 139 David wrote, "Where can I go from Your Spirit? Or where can I flee from Your presence?" (v. 7). Up to this point in the unfolding biblical revelation of God, the Trinity has not been made known to us fully as it will be in the New Testament. But in this passage, running away from God is said to be running away from the Spirit of God. Wherever anyone runs, there he will find the Holy Spirit present before his arrival.

So also the Old Testament asserts that the mighty power of the Holy Spirit was available to the people of God. In Zechariah, the angel who talked to him made this statement: "This is the word of the LORD to Zerubbabel: 'Not by might nor by power, but by My Spirit,' says the LORD of hosts" (Zech. 4:6). The mighty working power of the Holy Spirit was available to the people of God even as it is available to the saints in this age. This will be shown from the accounts of the lives of those on whom the Spirit came, enabling them to perform matchless and wonderful deeds beyond the ordinary powers of human beings.

The Israelites sinned against God again and again. The Scripture proclaims that in doing so they were sinning against the Holy Spirit. God spoke this word to Zechariah: The Israelites "made their hearts like flint, refusing to hear the law and the words which the LORD of hosts had sent by His Spirit through the former prophets. Thus great wrath came from the LORD of hosts" (Zech. 7:12). Then we learn that judgment fell. (It was the judgment of God the Father, not the judgment of the Holy Spirit, for that is not one of the stated works or functions of the Holy Spirit.) The Lord Almighty "scattered them with a whirlwind among all the nations which they had not known" (Zech. 7:14).

The people of Israel returned from captivity. The times were difficult and the rebuilding of the Lord's house remained uncompleted. Even when economic conditions improved and the people had occupied better homes, the house of God was still in ruins. Haggai called Israel to the task of rebuilding the temple. The message from God came to Israel through Him. God said, "Be strong, all you people of the land . . . and work; for I am with you. . . . According to the word that I covenanted with you when you came out of Egypt, so My Spirit remains among you; do not fear!" (Hag. 2:4,5).

Two points emerge from this statement. The first is that the Spirit of God was at work among the people of Israel when they came out of Egypt. He was leading and guiding them then. God said, secondly, that His Spirit was with them at that moment. It was the Spirit's will and power that was available to them when they were obedient to the command of God to rebuild the temple. The task could be accomplished because the power of the Spirit was there for them to use.

The general work of the Holy Spirit among God's people in the Old Testament period is readily perceived from the data of Scripture. But now we must look at the data about the work of the Holy Spirit in the lives of some of the people of God who were specially chosen by Him for service.

Here the work of the Holy Spirit should be seen within the context of endowment and enduement. By endowment we mean that the Holy Spirit gifted men and women with abilities He put into them at birth. These natural gifts were heightened and enlarged under the infilling power of the Holy Spirit. This is the enduement of the Spirit; that is, the manifestation of His divine power by which these gifts are used gloriously and successfully to accomplish the divine purpose. The Spirit brought to pass in the lives of God's servants those things that were in accord with the divine plan.

Moses

Moses was the great lawgiver, the political strategist, the moral leader of Israel, and the founding father of a great nation. He was singularly gifted by the Holy Spirit of God and then endued with mighty power that enabled him to perform the tasks he was given. It would have been humanly impossible for Moses to have served God among a disorganized and often disobedient people were it not for the divine power of the Spirit and the knowledge and wisdom that were apportioned to him. One significant incident in the life of Moses reveals the key to understanding the operation of the Spirit in his life and ministry.

During Israel's wilderness journey, a forty-year period brought about by their lack of faith in the sure Word of God, the people murmured and complained many times. In one incident they looked back with longing for the meat, cucumbers, melons, leeks, and garlic they had enjoyed in Egypt. They complained that they had nothing but manna from heaven, of which they had grown tired.

God had graciously provided manna for them day by day without their having to labor to obtain it. It was given without interruption, so that they never were threatened with famine on the journey. They had all they needed, so no one ever went hungry. The manna was dietetically excellent and met their physical needs in the best possible manner. The single drawback was that they had to eat the same food every day. The Israelites did not thank God for their blessings. Instead, they bemoaned their fate and made light of God's provisions for them. This brought anguish of spirit to Moses when the Israelites rebelled against him and despised his leadership.

No doubt Moses, from the human standpoint, had every reason to be depressed by the wickedness of Israel. As their leader he was the focal point of their dissatisfaction. The people, in effect, held him responsible for their sad state of affairs. Moses was so distressed that he began to complain against the God who had called him to serve and who had supported and sustained him all along the way. Moses' conversation with God revealed his own displeasure. He questioned the rightness and the goodness of the will of God for his life.

So Moses said to the LORD, "Why have You afflicted Your servant? And why have I not found favor in Your sight, that You have laid the burden of all these people on me? Did I conceive all these people? Did I beget them, that You should say to me, 'Carry them in your bosom, as a guardian carries a nursing child,' to the land which You swore to their fathers? Where am I to get meat to give to all these people? For they weep all over me, saying, 'Give us meat, that we may eat.' I am not able to bear all these people alone, because the burden is too heavy for me. If You treat me like this, please kill me here and now—if I have found favor in Your sight—and do not let me see my wretched-ness!" (Num. 11:11–15).

In his fit of depression, Moses himself brought charges against the God who had commissioned him. He alibied that God, not he, was responsible for giving birth to Israel. He thought God was unfair for giving him the sole responsibility for all of those people.

At this crisis-point in his leadership, he failed. Instead of drawing on the sufficient power and wisdom that God had given him to do the job, he looked to his flesh and admitted what was all too true. "I am not able to bear all these people alone." This was the speech of a man who, for the moment, had ceased to be dependent on God who had called him. He acted as though God had forsaken him. He invited God to kill him, implying that death was better than working for the God who had let him down. He was wrong in all of the points he made, however, because God had not forsaken him. Nor did God intend to forsake him. Moses erred in supposing that he was carrying the burden alone. Had not God given him His Holy Spirit? It was this truth Moses overlooked in this incident.

God dealt with Moses on the basis of his complaint:

So the LORD said to Moses: "Gather to Me seventy men of the elders of Israel, whom you know to be the elders of the people and officers over them; bring them to the tabernacle of meeting, that they may stand there with you. Then I will come down and talk with you there. I will take of the Spirit that is upon you and will put the same upon them; and they shall bear the burden of the people with you, that you may not bear it yourself alone" (Num. 11:16–17).

Moses had all of the Spirit and His power that he needed. Now that power was to be given to the seventy elders as well. There would be no additional power, for all the power that was necessary was already available to Moses. It was simply a real-location of the Spirit's power, not an increase of it. Moses brought the seventy elders to the Tent of Meeting. The Scripture then says, "The LORD came down in the cloud, and spoke to him, and took of the Spirit that was upon him, and placed the same upon the seventy elders; and it happened, when the Spirit rested upon them, that they prophesied, although they never did so again" (Num. 11:25).

In this account we are told that Eldad and Medad remained in the camp, even though they were listed among the elders, "And the Spirit rested upon them . . . [and] they prophesied in the camp" (Num. 11:26). A young man acquainted Moses with what had happened, and Joshua suggested to Moses that he should order them to stop prophesying. Moses answered, "Are you zealous for my sake? Oh, that all the LORD's people were prophets and that the LORD would put His Spirit upon them!" (Num. 11:29).

We may note from the conversation that special power or enduement of the Holy Spirit had come upon these elders as evidenced by the gift of prophecy that they exercised. Thus, there was outward confirming evidence that the power of the Holy Spirit was at work in them. Moreover, Moses suggests to us that in the Old Testament God sovereignly imparted His Spirit to whomever He was pleased to do so. This enduement was not something that was available to all the individuals of Israel, and it would not be available to all until Pentecost, when the church was born. Then, the Spirit would be poured out on all flesh.

Clearly Moses knew the Holy Spirit was at work within him. And the elders knew the Holy Spirit was at work in them. And to those on whom the Holy Spirit rested, there was given not only the power or enduement they needed but also the gifts or endowments essential to their ministry. The Holy Spirit was obviously operative in the life of Moses and through him in the life of Israel in that day.

Believers today should not miss the lesson we learn from this incident in the life of Moses. He had all the power he needed to do the job God had given to him. And God never gives anyone a job to do without giving the same person all of the power through the Spirit that is needed to finish the task. But to quit the task is sin. Moses was at fault here, and so will we be at fault if we faint and complain when the will of God seems too heavy for us to bear. At that moment we need instead to obey the promise that we can do all things through the One who strengthens us.

King Saul

When we think of the Spirit-filled believer in the Old Testament, King Saul stands out as one of sharp contrasts. His life is instructive because it was quite different from some of the other Spirit-filled lives we are considering. It presents us with an insight concerning the Spirit's working that enlarges our understanding in the specific area of sin that grieves or quenches the Holy Spirit.

God sovereignly determined to make Saul the king of Israel. This decision must be understood against the backdrop of Israel's repudiation of the theocracy in which God was King over His people. The Israelites determined to be like the other nations around them. They wanted a visible political symbol of rulership, not a spiritual reality that was perceived by faith and not by sight. In this they were no different from our own contemporary society, which is also secular, and just as committed to the visible as it is opposed to the invisible or spiritual. God agreed that He would provide Israel with a king, but at the same time He warned them of the consequences that would flow from this provision. Surely anything that displaces God as the supreme head is undesirable and in the end produces disastrous results.

God's call to Saul to be king was made known to him through Samuel the prophet. The order of events is fascinating. In 1 Samuel 8:19–22 we are told the following:

> The people refused to obey the voice of Samuel; and they said, "No, but we will have a king over us, that we also may be like all the nations, and that our king may judge us and go out before us and fight our battles." And Samuel heard all the words of the people, and he repeated them in the hearing of the LORD. So the LORD said to Samuel, "Heed their voice, and make them a king."

In 1 Samuel 9:15ff. we learn that "the LORD had told Samuel in his ear the day before Saul came, saying, 'Tomorrow about this time I will send you a man from the land of Benjamin, and you shall anoint him commander over My people Israel, that he may save My people from the hand of the Philistines; for I have looked upon My people, because their cry has come to me.'" Then in verse 17 the Scripture says, "There he is, the man of whom I spoke to you. This one shall reign over My people." In 1 Samuel 10:1 it is recorded that the prophet anointed Saul with oil, kissed him and said, "Is it not because the LORD has anointed you commander over His inheritance?"

In all of this God was the prime mover in the events. God told Samuel His choice for king. And when Samuel anointed Saul, he made it clear that it was God who had anointed Saul to be king even though it was Samuel who actually poured the oil on Saul's head and announced his coming reign.

Through Samuel, God provided Saul with outward confirming evidences by which he could know his appointment to the throne was truly from God and had His divine approval. Samuel told Saul the lost donkeys he was seeking would be found, three men would meet Saul, "one carrying three young goats, another carrying three loaves of bread, and another carrying a skin of wine. And they will greet you and give you two loaves of bread, which you shall receive from their hands" (1 Sam. 10:3–4). Saul was to go to Gibeah and, upon approaching the town, would see a procession of prophets coming down from the high place and engaged in prophesying. Then Samuel said, "The Spirit of the LORD will come upon you, and you will prophesy with them and be turned into another man. And let it be, when these signs come to you, that you do as the occasion demands; for God is with you" (1 Sam. 10:6–7).

From Saul's experience, several items of note emerge. The first is that God gave him external signs to show that Samuel's prophetic words were from God. Second, the Holy Spirit came upon him, both with regard to endowment for the office of king, and by giving him the divine power he needed to discharge his obligations. Third, Saul began to prophesy, showing others who had formerly known him that he was doing what God alone could make possible through His Holy Spirit. Fourth, he was changed into a different person. It is obvious, of course, what made the difference in the life of young Saul. It was the coming upon him of the Holy Spirit. Now he was equipped to be king over Israel. It was the Lord's doing and wonderful in everyone's sight.

The infilling of the Holy Spirit in the life of Saul, however, did not make him an automaton. He was still a responsible and a free agent. He could choose to do the will of God or refuse to obey Him. And his choices would be the result of his willingness to obey the knowledge he had as to what the will of God was. Later, Saul deliberately chose to disobey. God used Samuel to tell him that his kingship was to be ended and that another man would take his place.

In 1 Samuel 16:14 the desolating word manifests how God judged Saul: "But the Spirit of the LORD departed from Saul, and a distressing spirit from the LORD troubled him." Nothing

43

in the Scripture tells us what Saul's reaction was to the absence of the Holy Spirit in his life. And, quite differently from David at a later time, there is no reference to genuine repentance on the part of Saul. Moreover, when the Spirit of God left him, he was troubled by an evil spirit. The Scripture says it was "a distressing spirit from the Lord." Yes, even the evil spirits operate at the command of God. God freed this spirit to do his evil work in the heart and life of Israel's king. Certainly the sending of the evil spirit was the judgment of a just and a righteous God who warns us that a repudiation of the living God produces unhappy effects.

When He departed from Saul, however, the work of the Holy Spirit was not finished in Saul's life. After this the Spirit was to perform a work in him that was of a different nature. When Saul was busily engaged in seeking to capture and kill David, who was named by Samuel to be Saul's successor, he was informed that David was at Naioth at Ramah. He dispatched soldiers to capture him. "And when they saw the group of prophets prophesying, and Samuel standing as leader over them, the Spirit of God came upon the messengers of Saul, and they also prophesied" (1 Sam. 19:20). Saul was told about it, and he sent more men (not to prophesy but to take David captive so Saul could kill him), and they also prophesied. Saul sent a third contingent of soldiers, and they also prophesied. "So he [Saul] went there to Naioth in Ramah. Then the Spirit of God was upon him also, and he went on and prophesied until he came to Naioth in Ramah" (1 Sam. 19:23).

How are we to understand this unusual incident about Saul, from whom the Holy Spirit had departed earlier? Matthew Henry explains it this way:

When the messengers came into the congregation where David was among the prophets *the Spirit of God* came upon them, and *they prophesied,* that is, they joined with the rest in praising God. Instead of seizing David, they themselves were seized. . . . God secured David; for either they were put into such an ecstasy by the spirit of prophecy that they could not think of anything else, and so forgot their errand and never minded David, or they were by it put, for the present, into so good a frame that they could not entertain the thought of doing so bad a thing. . . . He (God through His Spirit) magnified his power over the spirits of men. He that made the heart and tongue can manage both to serve his own purposes. Balaam prophesied the happiness of Israel, whom he would have cursed; and some of the Jewish writers think these messengers prophesied the advancement of David to the throne of Israel.

Saul himself was likewise seized with the spirit of prophecy before he came to the place. One would have thought that so bad a man as he was in no danger of being turned into a prophet; yet, when God will take this way of protecting David, even Saul has no sooner come within the smell of the smoke of Naioth but he prophesies, as his messengers did. . . . He (Saul) is rejected of God, and actuated by an evil spirit, and yet among the prophets. [*Matthew Henry's Commentary* (Old Tappan, N.J.: Revell, n.d.), p. 388].

We are left to puzzle over the question whether Saul, who had sinned against God, was to die in an unregenerate state to be lost forever. Perhaps it is well for us to leave that at last in the hands of God, since there were others, such as Rahab who was a liar and Samson who was a fornicator and breaker of his Nazarite vows, who are spoken of favorably in Hebrews 11. And surely Ananias and Sapphira were numbered among the early believers in Acts 5, yet they were judged unto physical death for their lies against the Holy Spirit of God. The important lesson for us all, the matter that *is* clear, is that obedience to God throughout our lives brings with it lasting peace and the precious confidence of eternal reward.

David

David was a contemporary of Saul and his successor to the throne of Israel. He was said to be a man after God's own heart. God chose David to be the second king of Israel, even as He had chosen Saul before him.

David had a similar spiritual experience to that of Saul. He too was filled with the Holy Spirit. The mention of it comes in conjunction with the removal of the Holy Spirit from the life of Saul. David was chosen from among his brothers, although he was the youngest of them all. God looks on the heart, not on the outward appearance. And God saw in David what others might not have seen. Samuel, the Scripture says, "took the horn of oil and anointed him in the midst of his brothers; and the Spirit of the LORD came upon David from that day forward" (1 Sam. 16:13).

David's life-style subsequent to this experience testifies eloquently to the presence of the Holy Spirit in his life. Time and again he had the opportunity to kill Saul but he refrained from doing so. He understood that Saul was the Lord's anointed, and he knew that he had been ordained of God to succeed him in the kingship. He did not hasten the process, but left it in the hands of God, who puts up kings and brings them down at His good pleasure. He chose to wait on God rather than to use the arm of the flesh to accomplish what he knew to be the will of God for his life. Obviously he was under the control of the Holy Spirit.

The tragic moment in David's life came after Saul's death and his installation into his own kingship. His endeavors to defeat Israel's enemies succeeded. He was able to enlarge the kingdom and bring all of Israel under his royal control. Spring had come, "the time when kings go out to battle" (2 Sam. 11:1). On this occasion David "remained at Jerusalem." He chanced to walk about on the roof of the palace. As he glanced around he saw a beautiful woman bathing. He made inquiry and learned that she was Bathsheba, the wife of Uriah the Hittite, a faithful soldier in David's army. At that moment David had to make a decision between what he knew to be right and what he knew to be wrong. Even though he had been filled with the Holy Spirit, he did not choose to be led by the Spirit when he made his decision. He sent for Bathsheba to come to his palace.

Then Bathsheba was called upon to make her own choice. No doubt she was flattered that the king wanted her to visit him. But she knew the customs of the time. As a married woman whose husband was absent from the home on army duty, it was improper for her to go to the palace without an escort. It is futile to suppose that she did not suspect what the king might have had in mind when he invited her to come to him. Whether she did or not, she capitulated to his advances and engaged in the act of adultery.

Both of them sinned against God, and against their mates. They violated the law of God, which strongly forbade adultery, the penalty for which required that the guilty partners be stoned to death.

In due time Bathsheba informed David that she was pregnant, something that could only mean that she had acted adulterously, because her husband was still at war. At this point a repentant, Spirit-filled man would have acted differently. David, however, decided to protect himself and to see that Bathsheba was somehow delivered from her difficulty. He sought to have her husband go home to lie with her in an effort to provide legitimacy for the baby. But Uriah refused to visit his wife when the enemies of David were strong, and lying with his wife seemed to be inconsonant with his soldierly responsibilities. Defeated in this effort, David ordered that Uriah be put in the front line of the battle and then deserted so that he would be killed in action (see 2 Sam. 11).

God proceeded to deal with David because of his transgression. He sent the prophet Nathan to accuse David and to give him opportunity to repent. After a year of living a lie, David confessed his sin. The fifty-first Psalm records David's prayer concerning his wicked actions. In that Psalm David breathed forth the request, in which, following his repentance, he cried out, "Do not cast me away from Your presence,/And do not take Your Holy Spirit from me" (Ps. 51:11).

From this we may discern what David knew about the Holy Spirit and His operations. First, David knew there was a Holy Spirit. Second, he knew that he had been filled with the Holy Spirit. Third, he knew that it was possible for the Holy Spirit to leave him. He had seen this in the life of Saul whose decline rapidly followed the absence of the Holy Spirit from his life. Fourth, he knew that the loss of the Holy Spirit's presence was a disaster, and his better self revolted against the idea that the Spirit might depart from his life. Fifth, he knew that repentance and confession, followed by restoration, were part of the requirements of God for one on the road to recovery.

David was forgiven. There is no sad statement, such as was spoken about Saul, that the Holy Spirit had left him. But there was a pronouncement of judgment on David, by which he experienced the temporal consequences of his transgression in due season. He would remember what he had done long after the event had occurred. God decreed that David would feel the lash of divine judgment through his own family.

The child of the adulterous union died. Then, in the course of time Absalom, another dearly beloved son, embarked on a revolt against his father. Civil war ensued, and David was forced to flee from Jerusalem. The war continued, and at last the decisive battle was fought between the faithful troops of David and the army of Absalom. David was not at the battle and had given instructions for his army to treat his son tenderly. The news was brought to David that the battle was over and the civil war was ended. Immediately he inquired about his beloved Absalom. He was informed that Absalom was dead. The Scripture then says: "Then the king was deeply moved, and went up to the chamber over the gate, and wept. And as he went, he said thus: 'O my son Absalom—my son, my son Absalom—if only I had died in your place! O Absalom my son, my son!'" (2 Sam. 18:33).

David's grief for Absalom arose, in part, from the knowledge that he was, in some measure, responsible for what had happened. It brought back to his mind the decree of God against him when he had committed murder as well as adultery. The temporal effects of his transgression were felt by the desolated king. The Holy Spirit was not taken away from him as He was from Saul; indeed, the very holiness of the Spirit is highlighted in the life of David, who would have preferred his own death to the death of his son.

These things are written for our admonition. We learn from David's experience that those who have been filled with the Holy Spirit are not free to breach the laws of God. We are warned that the power of the Spirit may leave us if we willfully and persistently sin against His holiness. And these truths from the Old Testament have not been superseded or suspended by the Holy Spirit in the latter days.

THREE

The Holy Spirit,
the Judges, and the Prophets

In the last chapter, mention was made specifically about three of the major Old Testament characters: Moses, King Saul, and King David. Obviously, one would expect such people to be supernaturally assisted by God, for they occupied places of leadership. Moses, the great lawgiver, was the leader who brought the people of Israel out of bondage in Egypt. Saul and David were the first two kings of Israel and set contrasting patterns of leadership. And there were many others of whom the Old Testament Scriptures speak, who were filled with the Holy Spirit.

Judges, prophets, and other believers who were deeply involved in the life of Israel and in the coming of the Lord Jesus Christ, were filled with the Holy Spirit. The wide diversity of people so filled is an encouragement to every Christian today, for our fuller revelation states so clearly that there is nothing by way of the Spirit's power that is kept back from believers who want that power and are willing to meet the conditions whereby they may have it. We turn our attention first to one of the judges of the Old Testament.

Samson

Samson's life illustrates the infilling of the Holy Spirit from still other perspectives than some of those we have already mentioned. He was a Nazarite from birth, so no razor was to be used on his head and he was to drink no wine or other fermented drink. He was to eat nothing unclean.

Samson "grew, and the LORD blessed him. And the Spirit of the LORD began to move upon him at Mahaneh Dan between Zorah and Eshtaol" (Judg. 13:24–25). A young lion came roaring at him one time when he was in Timnath. The Bible says, "The Spirit of the LORD came mightily upon him, and he tore the lion apart as one would have torn apart a young goat, though he had nothing in his hand" (Judg. 14:6).

On another occasion he allowed the men of Judah to bind him with two new ropes. The waiting Philistines came out shouting. Then, "The Spirit of the LORD came mightily upon him" (Judg. 15:14). He broke the ropes, seized the jawbone of an ass, and with it slew a thousand Philistines. This was a mighty feat, which, from the human perspective, appears to have been an impossibility. The explanation for it comes from the fact that it was the Spirit of God who came upon him mightily and supplied him with the power he did not have in himself. With this power he was able to do what we regard as impossible.

The story of Samson also shows us how it was possible for a believer to lose the special enduement or power of the Holy Spirit. After he had consorted with Delilah, she managed to discover the source of his strength at last. It lay in his Nazarite vow. He was strong not *because* he drank no wine and allowed no razor to touch his head. Rather, these were the visible signs of his vow and commitment to God who made him strong. But the revealing of his spiritual secret and the cutting of his hair while he slept brought about his spiritual disaster. Delilah awakened him to tell him that the Philistines were coming after him as they had on other occasions when, in the power of the Spirit, he had prevented their taking him captive. It was the abandonment of his vow that brought about the breaking of his relationship to the living God through the power of the Holy Spirit. The words of Scripture here are among the saddest to be found in the Bible. Samson said, when Delilah awakened him: "I will go out as before, at other times, and shake myself free!" Then the calamitous statement follows: "But he did not know that the LORD had departed from him" (Judg. 16:20).

Samson, the man of power, was now powerless. The special power of God was gone from his life. The Spirit was quenched by his sin. The Philistines had no trouble taking him captive. They put out his eyes, bound him with bronze shackles, and set him to grinding in the prison (Judg. 16:21).

Samson had all the time in the world to ponder what he had done and to experience the consequences that flowed from his actions. He now knew that he had been a fool. He had sold his spiritual heritage for a bag of worms. It took time for his hair to grow. Meanwhile, he reflected on what he needed to do to restore his relationship to the living God and to experience the power of the Spirit in his life once more.

The final scene of Samson's life came when the Philistines gathered together in huge numbers to offer a great sacrifice to their god Dagon who, they thought, had given them the victory over Samson (see Judg. 16:23–25). God would teach us a lesson at this point. The victory of the Philistines over Samson was not due to the power of Dagon, nor did it mean that Dagon was greater than Samson's God. The fact is, it was not a conflict between God and Dagon. It was a conflict between Dagon and Samson, for God had left Samson to his own resources. Samson, without the power of the Spirit, was no stronger than any Philistine.

Samson's life teaches us still another helpful lesson. Samson came to himself. He knew the reason for his defeat. And he knew the way back to God is power. It was as it is today: the way of repentance, confession, and petition for restoration. Those who cry to God in true faith and repentance will not go unheeded. God is the God of grace. Hear then the prayer of Samson: "Oh Lord GOD, remember me, I pray! Strengthen me, I pray, just this once, O God, that I may with one blow take vengeance on the Philistines for my two eyes!" (Judg. 16:28).

Samson looked to the God of grace and power. He prayed the prayer of a penitent sinner. He humbly besought the Lord to restore his strength, knowing that God alone was the source of his power. Samson also prayed that he might die with the Philistines. God granted him both requests. The power came back.

In our mind's eye, we can see Samson flexing his muscles as he tested the pillars that held up the temple building in which three thousand Philistines were sporting as they praised their god Dagon. It was a moment of great import for Samson. Once more he knew what it meant to be obedient before God. Once more his Nazarite vow was central to his life. Once more the surging power of the Holy Spirit suffused his being. Once more he was the man he could have been all the days of his life.

He pushed with all his might and by the Spirit's power he was able to bring down the temple. God allowed him his revenge. He died as he did it. But in his death he slew more enemies of the living God than he had killed in all of his earlier days. Dagon was defeated. But he was not defeated by Samson. He was defeated by the God of glory whose power is greater than that of all the gods of this earth. God's name was vindicated, and the triumph of the Philistines was shortlived.

Does this not show us, by way of stark contrast, what is the difference between the Spirit-filled life and the backslidden walk of a spiritually defeated servant of God?

Bezaleel

In any discussion of the filling of the Holy Spirit, the Old Testament illustrations, for the most part, emphasize those who were prophets, kings, and great leaders of the people of God. The impression the evidence leaves, in general, would seem to support the conclusion that the Spirit only came upon extraordinary people and surely did not infill the common men and women of that day. But this conclusion is negated when we look at Bezaleel. His experience opens up for us the certainty that many people never mentioned in Scripture may well have been filled with the Holy Spirit.

Moses, in Exodus 31:1ff., recorded the outworking of God's will in the life of Bezaleel. Certain truths stand out like beacons that illumine the believer's pathway and encourage him or her to seek the filling of the Holy Spirit, whatever one's occupation or standing in life may be. First, Moses made it plain that God had chosen Bezaleel to be the leader of the workmen who were to construct the tabernacle. Bezaleel was given the requisite gifts. He was filled "with the Spirit of God, in wisdom, in understanding, in knowledge, and in all manner of workmanship, to design artistic works, to work in gold, in silver, in bronze . . ." (Ex. 31:3–4).

The Spirit of God who filled Bezaleel endowed him with the appropriate gifts and endued him with the power that would enable him to get the job done. Immediately we ask ourselves why the infilling of the Holy Spirit was necessary for *this* sort of work. It opens to us a larger picture than we sometimes perceive. Among the millions of believers in our generation, God has provided help for all to live constructively and to do noble works that will glorify Him. There is nothing any person can be or do that he cannot be and do better when filled with the Holy Spirit. The Spirit lifts believers to higher planes of life and service, by which they can do what they otherwise could never hope to accomplish.

There are gifts that the Holy Spirit wishes to give to believers. No one has the power he or she needs to make that gift or those gifts useful in the work of the kingdom unless filled with the Spirit. This may be understood in the context of the first question of The Larger Catechism: "What is the chief and highest end of man?" The answer is, "Man's chief and highest end is to glorify God, and fully to enjoy him for ever." No believer has glorified God the way he or she can do, unless he or she has been filled with the Holy Spirit. Those who really want to glorify God will want what God wants for all their lives. Bezaleel discovered this centuries ago.

The catechism's answer to the question of man's chief and highest end speaks to the other side of the equation. Whatever the believer does to glorify God will work for the believer's own good. No one who has not been filled with the Holy Spirit can fully enjoy God. Life is, and will be, different for the Spirit-filled child of God. The witness of all those who have tasted of this relationship confirms this viewpoint. Whoever wants maximum satisfaction in life, the highest sense of personal development, and the finest possible fellowship with the living God will find it when God is glorified. In sum, it may be said that the best way any believer can help him or herself is to glorify God.

Bezaleel's experience indicates that God is interested in those who can be used in every area of life. He gives gifts to those who wash dishes or scrub floors for His glory. He gives to some the ability to make money; to others the gifts required to be physicians, lawyers, or dentists. He gives to many women the gift of being wives and mothers in such a way that their husbands and children will be blessed and benefited as they would not be if their wives and mothers were not filled with the Spirit of God.

The Christian whose hands fashion beautiful works of art or whose fingers make musical instruments come alive may be likened to Bezaleel, to whom special gifts of craftsmanship were imparted by the Spirit for God's glory and for the good of God's people. More will be said later about the gifts of the

Spirit, many of which are unknown to some of the people of God. But they need to be known. The factory worker and the bus driver need to know what it means to glorify God through gifts like these.

Elijah and Elisha

No other persons in Scripture can be found who jointly had so magnificent a ministry as did Elijah and Elisha. Together they performed notable miracles and foretold things that came to pass. The gifts of prophecy and of performing miracles are gifts of the Holy Spirit.

Both of these prophets were filled with the Spirit. Had they not been, their pilgrimages would have been far different, for they would have lived on a lower spiritual plane than God intended. It is true that the Scriptures do not speak of the Spirit's infilling of these two prophets in as clear a fashion as they do about some of the others. But there is adequate evidence to convince us that they were both Spirit-filled men.

In the case of Elijah, there is one convincing statement that illustrates how he was infilled by the Spirit. The moment came when he was to speak to King Ahab face to face. In the third year of King Ahab's reign, "the word of the LORD came to Elijah . . . , saying, 'Go, present yourself to Ahab, and I will send rain on the earth'" (1 Kin. 18:1). Elijah, whose life was characterized by instant obedience, began moving toward his interview with King Ahab. As he went, he came into contact with the servant of King Ahab, Obadiah. The Word of God says that "Obadiah feared the LORD greatly" and that he "had taken one hundred prophets and hidden them, fifty to a cave, and had fed them with bread and water" (1 Kin. 18:3–4), thus saving them from death at the hands of Ahab's wife, Jezebel.

Here we should observe that Elijah was not the only prophet of God in that day. There were a hundred other prophets whose names have not been inscribed in the Bible. They were no less faithful than Elijah, and although they are not recorded as being as noteworthy as he was, we can be sure that, as true prophets, they too were filled with the Spirit. Thus, multiplied numbers of God's Spirit-filled people today may be unknown to the world. They are no less infilled and no less important in the total program of God than were these hundred prophets whose names we will learn in glory.

Obadiah had shielded these prophets against the wickedness of his master. Is it not wonderful that God placed faithful Obadiah in a position where he could aid the prophets of God and bring the wicked counsel of King Ahab to naught? When Elijah came face to face with Obadiah, the predicament of Obadiah became apparent. Elijah told him to go to King Ahab to inform him that the prophet himself was there.

Obadiah knew that his master had killed other prophets and had sought to kill Elijah too. He feared that if he brought this message to King Ahab, he too would be killed, for the king would be angry that he had not captured Elijah and brought him in to the king. Obadiah openly affirmed that he had worshiped the Lord since his youth. He also supposed that if he told King Ahab that he had seen Elijah, Elijah would disappear. Here it is that Obadiah's spiritual insight was manifested. He said, "And now you say, 'Go, tell your master, "Elijah is here"'! And it shall come to pass, as soon as I am gone from you, that the Spirit of the LORD will carry you to a place I do not know . . ." (1 Kin. 18:11–12).

Obadiah recognized that Elijah had the Holy Spirit. He knew that the Spirit of God was able to take Elijah wherever He wished. He knew that Elijah possessed what his master did not have. No one could have done what Elijah had done, and would do, unless he was filled with the Holy Spirit. So great was Elijah the prophet that it was prophesied in Malachi 4:5,

"Behold, I will send you Elijah the prophet
Before the coming of the great and dreadful day of the LORD.
And he will turn
The hearts of the fathers to the children,
And the hearts of the children to their fathers,
Lest I come and strike the earth with a curse."

Elijah is mentioned a number of times in the New Testament. The people of Jesus' day looked for the coming of Elijah. Jesus' disciples said, "Why then do the scribes say that Elijah must come first?" (Matt. 17:10). In response to this question Jesus said,

> "Elijah truly is coming first and will restore all things. But I say to you that Elijah has come already, and they do not know him but did to him whatever they wished. Likewise the Son of Man is also about to suffer at their hands." Then the disciples understood that He spoke to them of John the Baptist (Matt. 17:11–13).

Jesus' statement about Elijah in Matthew was occasioned by the appearance of Elijah at the transfiguration, which is reported in the same chapter. Elijah and Moses were together. They talked with Jesus. The disciples were so shaken they thought of building three shelters on the mountain, one for Jesus and one each for Moses and Elijah. No prophet in Israel exercised a greater influence than did Elijah, God's Spirit-filled servant, who won the victory over the priests of Baal and their god in the contest on Mount Carmel.

Elijah was succeeded by another notable prophet, Elisha. His call and ministry in some ways paralleled that of his mentor, Elijah. When the time had come for God to take Elijah to heaven (for he was not to die but to be translated) Elisha was appointed to be his successor. It was Elijah, himself, to whom God spoke. He ordered the prophet to anoint Elisha in his stead:

"You shall anoint Jehu the son of Nimshi as king over Israel. And Elisha the son of Shaphat of Abel Meholah you shall anoint as prophet in your place. . . ."

So he departed from there, and found Elisha the son of Shaphat. . . . Then Elijah passed by him and threw his mantle on him. And he left the oxen and ran after Elijah, and said, "Please let me kiss my father and my mother, and then I will follow you." And he said to him, "Go back again, for what have I done to you?" So Elisha turned back from him, and took a yoke of oxen and slaughtered them and boiled their flesh, using the oxen's equipment, and gave it to the people, and they ate. Then he arose and followed Elijah, and served him (1 Kin. 19:16, 19–21).

God is the one who calls whom He wants to His service as prophet. Elisha did not put himself forward. He may never even have dreamed that he might someday be a prophet of God. His response to the call of God was either to accept or to reject that call. His obedience, even though the call of God was administered through Elijah, was prompt and unquestioning. His desire to kiss his mother and father good-bye was no sign of hesitancy on his part. Rather, it signified that they would lose him from home and field forever. From that moment forward he would be fully dedicated to God.

Elisha became Elijah's attendant. There was a school of the prophets who were well acquainted with Elijah, but God did not choose one of them to succeed Elijah. He chose a novice who had not not been taught in the school of the prophets. God's ways are not our ways. But God knows what He is doing.

At last the time came for God to take Elijah up to heaven in a whirlwind (see 2 Kin. 2: 1–18). Prior to this, Elisha followed his master to the Jordan River:

And fifty men of the sons of the prophets went and stood facing them at a distance, while the two of them stood by the Jordan. Now Elijah took his mantle, rolled it up, and struck the water;

and it was divided this way and that, so that the two of them crossed over on dry ground. And so it was, when they had crossed over, that Elijah said to Elisha, "Ask! What may I do for you, before I am taken away from you?" And Elisha said, "Please let a double portion of your spirit be upon me." So he said, "You have asked a hard thing. Nevertheless, if you see me when I am taken from you, it shall be so for you; but if not, it shall not be so" (2 Kin. 2: 7–10).

What does the phrase "double portion of your spirit" mean? When we look at the context of the entire event, it becomes apparent that Elisha and the prophets had a good knowledge of the operations of the Holy Spirit. When Elijah was taken away from them, the event was witnessed by the company of the prophets. They had seen Elijah part the waters of the river Jordan. As soon as Elijah was taken away, Elisha picked up Elijah's cloak and struck the water of the river with it. The river parted for him as it had parted for Elijah, and he walked over without getting wet. The company of the prophets exclaimed, "The spirit of Elijah rests on Elisha" (2 Kin. 2:15). Then they said to Elisha, "Look now, there are fifty strong men with your servants. Please let them go and search for your master, lest perhaps the Spirit of the LORD has taken him up and cast him upon some mountain or into some valley" (2 Kin. 2:16).

The company of prophets believed in the miraculous. They attributed such power to the Spirit of God. Their acknowledgment that "The spirit of Elijah is resting on Elisha," may only be adequately interpreted as their affirmation that the same Spirit that had rested on Elijah was now resting on Elisha. To think it was something in Elijah himself, rather than the Spirit of God, does not follow. The fact that Elisha was able to part the waters of the Jordan demonstrated that he had Elijah's power. But what was that power? It was the power of the Spirit who infilled his life and equipped him for ministry. Matthew Henry sums up this point in the following way:

[Elisha] asks for the Spirit, not that the gifts and graces of the Spirit were in Elijah's power to give, therefore he says not, "Give me the Spirit" (he knew very well it was God's gift), but, "LET IT BE UPON ME, intercede with God for this for me." Christ bade his disciples ask what they would, not one, but all, and promised to send the Spirit, with much more authority and assurance than Elijah had (Ibid., p. 713).

In a secondary sense, we can assert that he also wanted the same kind of spirit that characterized the life and ministry of Elijah. After all, he was to take Elijah's place and carry on his work. He wanted a double portion of Elijah's spirit. He needed this if he were to meet and overcome similar obstacles such as Elijah faced. In other words, he wished to labor like Elijah, and he knew he needed more of what Elijah had, as compared to what the members of the school of the prophets had. Extra duties require extra support. To whom much is given by way of ministry, to them will God, by His Spirit, give the enduement to accomplish what they have been called to do.

Elisha performed more miracles, at least so far as the divine record is concerned, than did Elijah. When he died and was buried, there followed a unique miracle not elsewhere repeated in the lives of any of God's people in Scripture. A dead man's body was thrown into Elisha's tomb. As soon as the body touched the bones of Elisha, the man came back to life and stood up on his feet (2 Kin. 13:21).

The power that was manifested in the lives of Elijah and Elisha eloquently testifies to the work of the Holy Spirit in their lives. They were given the gift of being prophets, and they were empowered so that they could perform miracles and speak forth the true word of God to those to whom they ministered. This same Holy Spirit power is available to *all* of God's people since Pentecost.

Ezekiel

The prophet Ezekiel spoke more about the work of the Holy Spirit in his life than any other Old Testament prophet. Ezekiel exercised the office of prophet during the days of the Babylonian captivity. He was called by the Holy Spirit to do so in the fourth month of the fifth year of the captivity. He had been carried away to Babylon as a young man, a decade before the destruction of Jerusalem.

In chapter 2, verse 1, God spoke to Ezekiel, saying, "Son of man, stand on your feet, and I will speak to you." Then Ezekiel recorded a marvelous experience: "The Spirit entered me when he spoke to me, and set me on my feet" (v. 2). He continued in chapter 3:12–14, "Then the Spirit lifted me up, and as the glory of the LORD arose from its place, I heard behind me the sound of a great earthquake. . . . The Spirit lifted me up and took me away" (RSV). Ezekiel was being moved here and there by the power of the Holy Spirit, who took him wherever He wanted Ezekiel to go. In verse 24 of the same chapter, Ezekiel wrote, "Then the Spirit entered me and set me on my feet, and spoke with me and said to me: 'Go, shut yourself inside your house.'"

Later, Ezekiel had an extraordinary experience, somewhat analogous to Paul's, when he was lifted above the earth. Ezekiel wrote, "He stretched out the form of a hand, and took me by a lock of my hair; and the Spirit lifted me up between earth and heaven, and brought me in visions of God to Jerusalem, to the door of the north gate of the inner court, where the seat of the image of jealousy was, which provokes jealousy" (Ezek. 8:3). In 11:1 Ezekiel wrote, "Then the Spirit lifted me up and brought me to the east gate of the LORD's house." In 11:5 he wrote, "Then the Spirit of the LORD fell upon me." In 11:24 we find these words: "Then the Spirit took me up and brought me in a vision by the Spirit of God into Chaldea. . . ."

Toward the end of his prophecy, Ezekiel was still speaking about the operation of the Holy Spirit, who had come upon him again and again. This Spirit led him, lifted him up, spoke to him, gave him words to speak to the people, and in every way was the leading instrumentality in his life and pilgrimage. Announcing his vision of the future return of the Lord to the temple, Ezekiel said, "And the glory of the LORD came into the temple by way of the gate which faces toward the east. The Spirit lifted me up and brought me into the inner court; and behold, the glory of the LORD filled the temple" (43:4–5).

It is especially important for us to remember that Ezekiel was speaking about two of the three persons of the Trinity. He did not confuse them. It was the Spirit who lifted him up so that he could see the glory of the Lord. Through knowledge and experience he had a substantial amount of information about the Holy Spirit. Thus we know that the knowledge about the person and the work of the Holy Spirit, which would be increased greatly in the New Testament, was still considerable. The Spirit was at work mightily in His Old Testament servants.

Micah

The prophecy of Micah is contained in a short book of seven chapters. This flaming prophet of social righteousness pronounced definitive judgment on Judah and Israel. He was unsparing in his critique. He also made it clear that there were false prophets who were leading the people astray. Against this backdrop he made the following claim:

> But truly I am full of power
> by the Spirit of the LORD,
> And of justice and might,

To declare to Jacob his transgression
And to Israel his sin (Mic. 3:8).

From this it is clear that Micah experienced the power of the Holy Spirit in his life, and acknowledged that the message he uttered about the sins of Jacob and Israel came from the Spirit. No false prophet could make any claim like this. It may well be that others of the minor prophets, who did not specifically mention the Holy Spirit, nevertheless witnessed to His work, which they ascribed to the Lord God. For the Lord God worked through His Spirit who, as His agent, could be construed as doing what is attributed to the one who sent Him.

As we look at this Old Testament record of the judges and prophets and how they were moved by the Holy Spirit, we are both motivated by the miracles God can do and cautioned toward order in the body of Jesus Christ today.

FOUR

From the Old Covenant to the New

In the New Testament we have the witness and testimony to the work of the Holy Spirit in the lives of those who were pre-Pentecost illustrations of what it meant to be filled with the Holy Spirit of God. One of the most notable illustrations is that of a godly family, all of whose members were filled with the Holy Spirit. With this filling they were mightily used by God in the outworking of His plan of salvation. I have in mind Zacharias, Elizabeth, and their son John.

John the Baptist

When the angel Gabriel appeared to Zacharias to announce the birth of a son who was to be called John, the angel said that John "will also be filled with the Holy Spirit, even from his mother's womb" (Luke 1:15). This statement has implications we dare not overlook. It is quite clear that no one can be filled with the Holy Spirit who has not been regenerated. The Scripture proclaims that John would be Spirit-filled from his very birth. This means he must have been regenerated by the Holy Spirit while he was a fetus in his mother's womb.

Believers who favor, or are soft on, abortion should examine this Scripture carefully, for it has implications about taking the life of a fetus. Suppose that John had been aborted? This would have brought to naught the counsel of God, and this cannot be. John was filled with the Holy Spirit, and although the length of his ministry was short, he was the forerunner of Jesus. He played so significant a role that Jesus was to say, "among those born of women there is not a greater prophet than John the Baptist" (Luke 7:28).

Most people are filled with the Spirit after, not before, they are born into this world physically. In John's case a miracle occurred that constitutes an exception. It was not the general rule. An omnipotent God indeed can regenerate a human soul by the Spirit while it still is in embryo form. On the one hand, we should beware of building a theology of spiritual life based upon an isolated case. Neither should we run away from this notable exception or try to explain it away. It is a monument to the sovereign power of our great God, before whom we stand in awe and amazement. His ways are not our ways. John was Spirit-filled. So was his mother, Elizabeth.

Elizabeth

The only Gospel writer who speaks about the birth of John is Luke. His lovely account supplies us with facts we would not otherwise have known. Some of the details connected with the birth of John and the incarnation of Jesus are of such a nature that one can only suppose they were made available to Luke by the Holy Spirit Himself, who is the divine author of the written Word of God.

The incident concerning Elizabeth and her filling by the Holy Spirit occurred when Mary, to whom the angel Gabriel had revealed that by the will of God she should bear the Son of God, visited Elizabeth, her cousin, in the hill country of Judah. Mary was from the tribe of Judah. Elizabeth was from the tribe of Levi. How then could she have been a cousin of Elizabeth?

There was intermarriage between members of the tribes of Levi and Judah.

Following the angel Gabriel's visit, Mary hastened to visit Elizabeth, who also had become pregnant in a miraculous fashion, for she, like Sarah of old, was beyond the age when women become pregnant.

When Mary arrived at Elizabeth's house, she greeted her cousin, who, of course, did not know Mary was coming. What a happy moment when these two women, singularly blessed by God, could share their happiness with each other, knowing that both had been the subjects of the miracle-working power of the living God. Luke tells us that when Mary greeted Elizabeth, John leaped in his mother's womb. This must have been an extraordinary incident to have been mentioned in the way it appears. But what is even more important is that at that moment, Elizabeth was filled with the Holy Spirit (see Luke 1:41). Thus, we have John the fetus filled with the Spirit, and the mother who bore him likewise filled. But Elizabeth was also given knowledge by the Holy Spirit that defies human explanation. She was given the prophetic gift that enabled her to pronounce the divine word that Mary was blessed among all women and so was the fruit of her womb. Then follow the glorious words, "But why is this granted me, that the mother of my Lord should come to me?" (Luke 1:43).

Elizabeth was shown by the Holy Spirit that the babe in Mary's womb was her Lord, the Messiah promised ages before by the prophets. Even as Elizabeth knew she was with child in miraculous fashion, so she also knew that the Virgin Mary was with child by the Holy Spirit. She knew that the child in Mary's womb was the Lord Jesus, who would be both God and man. Elizabeth shouted those words with gladness and exclaimed that the babe in her own womb had leaped for joy.

Who knows in the providence of God what prenatal influence can come upon a fetus when the Holy Spirit of God is at work? And what better birth prospects could there be for any baby whose mother is filled with the Holy Spirit? Is this not the best guarantee that any child so born will be blessed and used by God for His glory?

Mary

But what about Mary herself, and the babe in her womb? The Scripture does not inform us about the intimate details of Mary's conception of Jesus. A holy veil of silence overshadows the entire event. All we know is that the angel told Mary, "The Holy Spirit will come upon you, and the power of the Highest will overshadow you" (Luke 1:35). Surely the Spirit who came upon Mary in life conceiving power, also came upon her in filling and prophesying power. Her song was revelatory, coming from the Spirit who gave her the words to speak. She magnified the name of God and rejoiced in Jesus whom she proclaimed to be *her* Savior too. She rejoiced that what God had promised the ancient fathers beginning with Adam and had made plain to Abraham had now come to pass. The Messiah was in the virgin's womb. God had remembered to show mercy, and sinners could rejoice that the sin-bearer who would remove their transgressions would soon be born and dwell among them.

Mary returned home after her visit with Elizabeth to await the birth of her son, who would be six months younger than John. Following her return to Nazareth, Luke wrote of the birth of John and the role of his father, Zacharias, who was sentenced to be dumb until the baby's arrival.

Zacharias

The angel Gabriel had brought to Zacharias the news of God's intention to allow Elizabeth to be the mother of John, the one chosen to prepare the way for the Messiah (see Luke 1:5–25).

Zacharias found it difficult to accept the incredible. His was a doubting faith. He was a true believer, but his faith was small, so far as it concerned the birth of a son by a wife who was long past menopause. Somehow he did not lay hold of the great biblical teaching that with God nothing is impossible. Thus he was sentenced to silence for his lack of faith. But by the time the baby was born, Zacharias had had nine long months to ponder his unbelief, to make his peace with God, and to await the coming of that blessed son who would be identified as the forerunner of the Messiah.

The relatives and neighbors could not accept the name of John for the baby, even though his mother had said what the boy's name was to be (see Luke 1:59–66). So they signaled to Zacharias. He wrote on a piece of paper the name *John*. When this occurred, Zacharias was released from his dumbness. And, glory of glory, he was filled with the Holy Spirit. He began to prophesy.

We remember how when Saul, the first king of Israel, began to prophesy when he was filled with the Holy Spirit. The by-standers in Saul's day wondered at the miracle that Saul had become a prophet. And no doubt the bystanders at the birth of John wondered about the gracious words that flowed from the mouth of a priest who, for many years, had performed his labors at the temple. Probably Zacharias had never uttered a prophetic word before this. The Holy Spirit loosened his tongue, enlightened his eyes, and mended his mind. He was God's mouthpiece, who spoke the prophetic Word of God. But he did it because he had been given the gift of prophecy and the power to say it by the Holy Spirit.

Zacharias proclaimed that God had visited and redeemed his people. A horn of salvation had been raised up in David's house. Israel was saved from her enemies and this had come through the promise of the covenant-keeping God. God committed Himself by an oath to Abraham to deliver His people so they could serve Him in holiness and righteousness, without fear. And Zacharias's own son, John, was to be called the prophet of the Most High, going before the Lord to prepare His way. The Dayspring was about to visit from on high, to give light to those who sat in darkness and in the shadow of death.

So spoke Zacharias under the inspiration of the Holy Spirit. Certainly this family was specially favored by God. The father was a priest of God serving in the Temple. The mother was honored by God through a miracle of conception. And John was the forerunner of the Lord. The three members of this family were filled with the Holy Spirit.

Simeon

There is one other pre-Pentecost or Old Testament saint we should mention as well. That is Simeon, who was a devout man of special distinction.

As far as I know, Simeon is mentioned only once in the Bible. This is in connection with the presentation of Jesus in the temple, to fulfill the requirements of the law about the firstborn male and for the rite of purification for Mary (see Luke 2:25–35). We learn from the account that Mary and Joseph were of modest means, because they brought for the offering either two turtledoves or two pigeons. Leviticus 12:8 says about the mother, "And if she is not able to bring a lamb, then she may bring two turtledoves or two young pigeons— one as a burnt offering and the other as a sin offering."

Luke wrote four things about Simeon. First, he was righteous, and second, devout. He was rightly related to God through saving faith. His life and personal witness indicated that he was not only a believer, but faithful. Third, he was looking for the consolation of Israel. In other words, he was waiting with expectancy for the coming of the Messiah, and in the light of this hope, he spent his time and gave his attention to the worship of God in the temple. Fourth, Simeon was filled with the Holy Spirit.

Three gracious truths are taught us about the Holy Spirit in this passage. They are important, not only because they teach us something about Simeon but also because they have a definite bearing on the lives of all believers today who want the will of God. The Holy Spirit is the believer's Helper. The first truth about the Spirit from Simeon's life is that He leads the people of God on their pilgrim journey. Sometimes the Spirit propels believers forward and sometimes He restrains them.

Paul and Barnabas offer a practical lesson for us all. They were busy at work for Jesus, preaching everywhere they could. They wanted to preach the gospel in Asia. But the Scripture says "they were forbidden by the Holy Spirit to preach the word in Asia." Then "they tried to go into Bithynia, but the Spirit did not permit them" (Acts 16:6,7). After that they had a vision of the man from Macedonia and discovered that going there was the will of the Holy Spirit for them (see Acts 16:9–10). Earlier, as recorded in Acts 13, Paul and Barnabas had been set apart by the church for missionary outreach. The Scripture specifically says that "being sent out by the Holy Spirit, they went down to Seleucia, and from there they sailed to Cyprus" (Acts 13:4).

Peter had an interesting experience in the form of a vision he had while praying, in which he was told that the Jewish prohibitions about certain meats were no longer to be practiced (see Acts 10:9–16). But what was most illuminating was what followed. As he was thinking about the vision, the Scripture says, "the Spirit said to him, 'Behold, three men are seeking you. Arise therefore, go down and go with them, doubting nothing;

73

for I have sent them'" (Acts 10:19–20). So Peter went as he was directed by the Spirit, and thus was the mission to the Gentiles begun (see Acts 10:24–48).

Simeon "came by the Spirit into the temple" (Luke 2:27). And Jesus was "led by the Spirit into the wilderness" (Luke 4:1). Thus, the experience of Simeon's being led by the Spirit was commonplace in the Scriptures and is just as true today as it was in bygone years. Charles E. Fuller was led by the Spirit to start the *Old Fashioned Revival Hour* and was assured it would become a worldwide radio broadcast of the gospel. Billy Graham was led by the Spirit to go to the Soviet Union to preach the gospel. It became a controversial matter, but there can be no doubt that he believed it was the Spirit of God who led him to go there. Thus, when Paul spoke about being led by the Spirit (see Rom. 8:14 and Gal. 5:18), he was laying down an important principle for all believers. We are to obey the Holy Spirit even when other believers do not understand. It is not the will of the Spirit for me to know His will for anyone other than myself, unless the same Spirit expressly teaches me otherwise.

The second great truth that comes to us from Simeon's life is that the Holy Spirit is our teacher. This is affirmed by Jesus, who said, "the Holy Spirit . . . will teach you all things" (John 14:26). Simeon knew the Old Testament Scriptures and was taught by the Spirit about the coming Messiah. Thus he looked for the consolation of Israel. But there was more to his experience than that. He had been told by the Holy Spirit that he would not die until he saw the Lord's Christ (see Luke 2:26).

The Holy Spirit is the divine author of Scripture. All Scripture is God-breathed through the Holy Spirit. But the canon of Scripture is closed. We have a back cover on the Bible. There is no more to be given. Does this mean there is no possibility of the Spirit's giving a word of knowledge or a word of prophecy to His people today? Here we need to be careful, for such a notion is subject to misuse and serious abuse. But that possibility should not cause us to suppose that the same Holy Spirit who was at work in the writing of the Old and the New Testaments no longer works in this manner today.

A. T. Pierson, in his book *The New Acts of the Apostles*, tells the story about Hans Egede and his wife. They went to Greenland to work among the Eskimos and discovered they needed supernatural signs to break through the wickedness, the apathy, and the degradation of the people. Pierson says, "feeling that only some sure sign of Divine power could melt their stolid apathy, Egede boldly asked for the gift of healing, and was permitted in scores of cases to exercise it, while his wife received the gift of prophecy, predicting, in the crisis of famine, the very day and hour when a ship should come bearing supplies" (p. 84).

King David professed to be taught by the Spirit. He said, "The Spirit of the LORD spoke by me, and His word was on my tongue" (2 Sam. 23:2). He indeed was taught by the Spirit. Saul was David's predecessor and of him the Scripture says, when the Spirit came upon him he was changed into a different person. He was given another heart. We learn that "the Spirit of God came upon him, and he prophesied among them" (1 Sam. 10:10).

The Old Testament is filled with examples of prophets who were taught by the Spirit: Isaiah, Ezekiel, Daniel, Hosea, Joel, Micah, Haggai, and Zechariah. Just as these Old Testament believers were taught by the Spirit, so believers today have the same privilege and right. While it is true that the Spirit ordinarily teaches us from the written Word of God, it is also true that He can and does teach us in other ways and about other things in our own personal experiences. These never conflict with or contradict the Scriptures, nor do they constitute new Scripture. But they are part of the ongoing work of the Spirit, who should not be handcuffed or limited or boxed in by human ideas for which there is no explicit warrant from the Bible itself.

The third truth we perceive from the life of Simeon has to do with being filled with the Holy Spirit. This is what supplies us with the dynamite of God we all need to make our witness and our words powerful. Simeon, according to tradition, may have been the son of Hillel, whom he succeeded as president of the college his father founded. He would then have been the head of the Sanhedrin. The Jews of his day affirmed that he was endued with a prophetical spirit. His spiritual life was such that he was both taught and led by the Spirit. But best of all, he was filled with the Holy Spirit, and this latter fact is what marks off his powerful influence and the role he played in the presentation of Jesus at the temple.

Through the ages one fact stands out starkly: virtually without exception there has never been a man or a woman of God who performed great exploits for God who was not filled with the Spirit. This is true in Scripture. And it is also true in the history of the Christian church through the ages. Moody was Spirit-filled. Torrey was Spirit-filled. Finney was Spirit-filled. Graham is Spirit-filled. Hosts of God's servants this very hour have been filled with the Holy Spirit. The lesson from Simeon's life is plain. He had what we all need. He had what we all can have. The power of the infilling of the Spirit is what makes the difference between a life of ordinary service and a supercharged life that brings victory after victory for the glory of God.

On to Pentecost

There are many other places in the Old Testament in which references are made to the work of the Holy Spirit. What we have seen thus far reveals what the work of the Holy Spirit was before Pentecost. His work in Old Testament times was somewhat different from what He does now that Christ has been glorified and is seated at the right hand of the Father in heaven. Since Pentecost, with the beginning of the latter days, believers live in the age of the Holy Spirit, who proceeds from the Father and is sent by the Father and the Son. Once the atoning work of the Son was completed and His sacrifice was accepted by the Father in the heavenly sanctuary where His finished work is magnified, the time was ripe for the Holy Spirit's advent.

What is the Spirit doing now, and how does His present work relate to the living of the Christian life? Is there something the Holy Spirit brings into the lives of the people of God that does not come automatically but is received by any believer who meets the conditions? If this be so, what are the conditions that must be met to receive the full riches of the Spirit's presence and work, and how do we know that we have the fullness we all should desire and seek?

Those are some of the important questions to which we turn our attention, seeking the light the Holy Spirit alone can bring and claiming the promise that He will teach us all things.

FIVE

Pentecost

We have seen how the Holy Spirit worked in the lives of many of God's servants in the Old Testament. He came upon those people at His good pleasure, to accomplish what was in accord with the plan of God for human salvation.

The revelation of God is progressive. Many things not known about God were revealed to men and women during the Old Testament period. But when the revelation of God in the Old Testament was finished it was not the end of revelation. More was yet to come. The New Testament age lay ahead in the plan of God.

We learn from the Old Testament that the Holy Spirit was the divine author of the Word of God. It was the Holy Spirit who enabled the prophets to speak the truth with boldness. It was the Holy Spirit who spoke through David, king of Israel. It was the Holy Spirit who gave King Saul the gift of prophecy when He came upon him. It was the Holy Spirit who empowered Samson, so that he overcame the Philistines. It was the Holy Spirit who gave Bezaleel the gifts and the power to build the tabernacle.

We have also seen how the Holy Spirit came and departed at His own good pleasure. He left Samson when his Nazarite vow was broken. He left Saul when he failed to obey the commandment of the Lord. He remained with David after his adultery with Bathsheba and the murder of her husband, Uriah, but this occurred only because David repented, confessed his sins, turned from his wicked ways, and prayed in faith that the Holy Spirit would remain with him.

When we come to the New Testament, we are told by Paul that believers are sealed by the Holy Spirit. He said, "In Him [Christ] . . . also, having believed, you were sealed with the Holy Spirit of promise" (Eph. 1:13). And this sealing of the Holy Spirit "is the guarantee of our inheritance until the redemption of the purchased possession, to the praise of His glory" (v. 14). Were the Old Testament saints sealed by the Holy Spirit? If so, how does what we know as sealing of the Spirit in our lives today, differ from their experience?

Sealing

The use of seals was an ancient custom. One of the uses of a seal was to identify the ownership of property. Wills, too, were sealed. An even older custom was to seal or brand animals to identify ownership. Human slaves were also marked or sealed by piercing the ear or branding.

It is against the background of this sort that the sealing of the Holy Spirit is to be understood. God seals believers by His Spirit when they are baptized into the body of Christ. Those thus sealed now belong to Him and His mark is placed upon them to identify them and to certify that they belong to God by purchase through redemption.

Perhaps the life of Abraham affords a clue about the sealing and indwelling of the Holy Spirit in the lives of the Old Testament saints. He is a key figure in Pauline theology with regard to justification by faith through the death of Christ on Calvary. Paul declares that Abraham was justified before Calvary. How can this be understood?

Abraham, by faith, looked forward to Calvary in the promise

of God made to Him. By that faith he was declared to be righteous. Yet he saw through the mirror darkly. He did not have all of the information about the Messiah we have now. Although he was limited in knowledge, the saving reality was no less genuine.

The Abrahamic analogy with regard to justification can be applied to the person and work of the Holy Spirit. We know we have been sealed and are indwelt by the Spirit. It is my opinion that Abraham, likewise, was sealed and indwelt by the Spirit. God's mark was certainly upon him, and he did God's will.

I also believe one can possess the presence of the Holy Spirit and not always know it. Indeed multitudes of people who profess Christ for salvation now do not know they have been sealed and indwelt by the Spirit. And some believers have died in the age since Pentecost without any more awareness of these facts than perhaps even Abraham possessed.

When we get to the New Testament record, the whole matter of the sealing of the Spirit becomes clear. Paul wrote, "In Him you also trusted, after you heard the word of truth, the gospel of your salvation; in whom also, having believed, you were sealed with the Holy Spirit of promise" (Eph. 1:13).

Today believers have the complete written revelation of God, the Old and New Testament Scriptures. No signs are required for us to know we have been sealed and indwelt by the Spirit. But when it comes to the gifts and power of the Spirit (being filled or baptized with the Spirit), we have another aspect of the work of the Spirit, which sometimes produces visible effects.

The Pre-Pentecost Promise of the Spirit

In the prophecy of Joel the coming of the Holy Spirit is promised clearly. And Peter specifically stated later that

Pentecost was the fulfillment of this prophecy (see Acts 2:14–21).

Joel said,

And it shall come to pass afterward
That I will pour out My Spirit upon all flesh.
Your sons and daughters shall prophesy,
Your old men shall dream dreams,
Your young men shall see visions;
And also on My menservants and on My maidservants
I will pour out My Spirit in those days (Joel 2:28–29).

Jesus also spoke about the coming of the Spirit at Pentecost. One account in John's Gospel is clarified by John because the statement of Jesus is not clear enough for uninstructed readers to comprehend. John first wrote, "On the last day, that great day of the feast, Jesus stood and cried out, saying, 'If anyone thirsts, let him come to Me and drink. He who believes in Me, as the Scripture has said, out of his heart will flow rivers of living water'" (John 7:37–38). But what did Jesus mean? And to what Scripture was He referring when He said, "as the Scripture has said"? Evidently He was speaking about the prophecy of Joel. John went on to make clear to us what Jesus was talking about. He wrote, "But this He spoke concerning the Spirit, whom those believing in Him would receive; for the Holy Spirit was not yet given, because Jesus was not yet glorified" (John 7:39).

From this Scripture we learn that Pentecost would come *after* Jesus was glorified. His death, resurrection, and glorification lay before Him. And after all these things had taken place, the Spirit of God would come. Second, we learn that we must receive the Holy Spirit. And third, we learn that when we have received the Holy Spirit we will have access to rivers of living water that will flow out from us.

This figure of speech is graphic. It speaks of a state of being that should be the desire of every born-again child of God. Every believer should desire, and can have, rivers of living water flowing out of him or her. Rivers and water are often metaphors in Scripture for the Holy Spirit. In this illustration, Jesus is talking about life in the Spirit as more than the human "river bed" can contain. We are to overflow, as it were, with spiritual life. And obviously one who has rivers of living water flowing from within him would be conscious of that fact. Yet many believers who have been sealed and indwelt know nothing of the rivers of living water of which Jesus spoke.

Receiving the Holy Spirit

Both Matthew and Luke recorded the saying of Jesus about prayer that reads, "Ask, and it will be given to you. Seek, and you will find. Knock, and it will be opened to you" (Matt. 7:7; Luke 11:9). Both continued, elucidating the meaning of this statement, but Luke threw light on one aspect of it that Matthew did not mention. He wrote the following words: "If you then, being evil, know how to give good gifts to your children, how much more will your heavenly Father give *the Holy Spirit* to those who ask Him!" (Luke 11:13, italics mine).

We learn from this something about the availability of the Holy Spirit to the children of God. They are told to ask the Father for this gift of the Holy Spirit. This Scripture must be understood properly. Does Jesus' statement refer to Pentecost itself? If it does, then no believer today needs to ask the heavenly Father to give him the Holy Spirit. Indeed, he should carefully refrain from doing so. On the other hand, if this Scripture is applicable for *us* and was not written simply for *them*, then it refers to something we need and ought to have beyond being sealed and indwelt by the Spirit. What happened subsequent to Pentecost supports the notion that this Scripture is for us now.

So great will the power of the Holy Spirit be in the lives of the people of God that, "when they bring you to the synagogues and magistrates and authorities, do not worry about how or what you should answer, or what you should say. For the Holy Spirit will teach you in that very hour what you ought to say" (Luke 12:11–12). Thus, the Holy Spirit is to be our teacher as well as our filler and empowerer.

Luke also recorded for us the words of Jesus about the coming of the Holy Spirit after the resurrection. The Great Commission is found in Luke 24:45–48. Attached to that is the word of Jesus about the Holy Spirit. He said, "Behold, I send the Promise of My Father upon you; but tarry in the city of Jerusalem until you are endued with power from on high" (Luke 24:49). Luke carried on with this theme in the Acts of the Apostles, which he also wrote. In chapter 1 he said that Jesus, "through the Holy Spirit had given commandments to the apostles whom He had chosen" (Acts 1:2). One of these commandments was that they were to "wait for the Promise of the Father, 'which,' He said, 'you have heard from Me; for John truly baptized with water, but you shall be baptized with the Holy Spirit not many days from now'" (Acts 1:4–5).

The Signs of the Spirit's Coming

We come now to Pentecost itself. Luke wrote about the event as a day that had "fully come" (see Acts 2:1). The event had been planned by God from before creation itself. Pentecost could not take place before the time ordained by God. And whatever needed to transpire prior to Pentecost had first to take place. The coming of the Spirit was imminent. The Scriptures reveal that at every major turning point in the history of salvation, God gave external corroborating signs by which the people of God could know that what had happened was from God.

During the time of Elijah, Israel was worshiping Baal instead of Jehovah. The priests of Baal had attained political ascendancy. Elijah called upon Israel to be faithful to Jehovah. He boldly challenged the priests of Baal to come to Mount Carmel to offer their sacrifices and he would offer his. The challenge was plain. Whichever god responded by sending fire from heaven to consume the sacrifice would be acknowledged to be the true God.

The priests of Baal did everything within their power to call down the fire from heaven. But their sacrifices were not consumed. Elijah mocked them. He asked whether their god was asleep. Then he made ready his sacrifice. He went so far as to douse his sacrifice with much water. And when he called upon Jehovah, He answered with fire from heaven that consumed Elijah's sacrifice. The people of Israel had external corroborating evidence by which they knew whether Baal or Jehovah was the true God.

So also did God make known to all that Jesus was the true Messiah, the redeemer of the world. At His birth there were the shepherds and the wise men; there was the star in the sky and the song of the angels. There was the fulfillment of the prophetic word that Jesus would be born in Bethlehem of Judea. When Jesus was baptized, the Holy Spirit appeared in the form of a dove and the voice of the Father from heaven proclaimed that Jesus was His Son. Jesus Himself informed people how they could know He was the Son of God. He asserted that if they did not believe His words they should look at His works. They certified that His words were true. He performed mighty miracles including the raising of the dead. When He rose from the dead, He appeared to His disciples who then had personal proof that He was alive forevermore.

It was just as essential at Pentecost, when the church was born and the disciples were filled with the Holy Spirit, that there should be outward, confirming signs. By them, the disciples would know the new age had begun and that what Jesus had prophesied had really come to pass.

The Background for Pentecost

Pentecost was close at hand. Jesus had risen from the dead. Had there been no resurrection there could have been no Pentecost. Moreover, if there was no real resurrection of the body of Jesus from the tomb, the Pentecost event would have lost its meaning. For our union with the living Christ and the fullness of the Holy Spirit go hand in hand. The great fact behind Pentecost was that Jesus, who had died, was alive forevermore.

Following the resurrection, forty-nine days came and went before the advent of the Holy Spirit. Even as there was the first advent of Jesus when He became flesh and dwelt among us, so there had to be an advent of the Holy Spirit, who would come to be the representative of the risen and ascended Christ.

Since the grave could not contain Jesus, why did He not ascend at once into heaven, instead of tarrying for forty days? There are several reasons. The first is that those in the community of faith would be able to see Him, hear Him, touch Him, and eat with Him. His was a resurrection body. But it was the same body that had taken on immortality.

Jesus also tarried to instruct His disciples. He made known to them not only all things concerning Himself from the Old Testament but also gave them what we call the Great Commission. This constitutes the marching orders of the church until Jesus appears the second time in power and great glory. This commission is recorded once in each of the four Gospels and the fifth time in the Acts of the Apostles. We will limit ourselves to what is reported by Luke in the Acts.

The disciples, despite the forty days of teaching by Jesus, still did not grasp fully what He had told them in His Great

Commission prior to the day of His ascension. Just before Jesus left this earth for heaven, the disciples asked Him if He would "at this time restore the kingdom to Israel" (Acts 1:6). Jesus brushed this question aside and said, "But you shall receive power when the Holy Spirit has come upon you; and you shall be my witnesses in Jerusalem and in all Judea and Samaria and to the end of the earth" (Acts 1:8 RSV).

It is helpful to note that only Luke made specific reference to power and to the Holy Spirit in relation to Pentecost. In his Gospel, Luke recorded Jesus as saying, ". . . stay . . . until you are clothed with power from on high" (Luke 24:49 RSV). Although he did not mention the Holy Spirit specifically in this verse, He was there implicitly. In the Acts of the Apostles, however, Luke recorded two definite and specific statements about the Holy Spirit from the lips of the Master: "You shall be baptized with the Holy Spirit" (Acts 1:5), and "you shall receive power when the Holy Spirit has come upon you" (Acts 1:8).

Following the ascension, the disciples, together with approximately one hundred and twenty other people, waited for ten days. And while they waited they were of one accord, and they "devoted themselves to prayer" (Acts 1:14 RSV). This surely must be called one of the most important prayer meetings recorded in the Word of God. They were expectant because they had the word of Jesus that the Spirit would come. They knew that He would give them the power they needed to do the work of God.

Then the day of Pentecost came. The disciples of Jesus did not know what to expect, nor did they know in advance the details about all of the things that would happen to them.

The Experience of Pentecost

The Pentecost event was marked by four confirming signs. The first was the sound from heaven "as of a rushing mighty wind" that "filled the whole house where they were sitting" (Acts 2:2). Second, "there appeared to them divided tongues, as of fire, and one sat upon each of them" (v. 3). None of them lacked this sign. The cloven tongues sat upon each and every one of them. Third, they all spoke in tongues (see v. 4). The fourth sign that Pentecost had come was that they were all filled with the Holy Spirit.

Our first concern here has to do with the "baptism with the Holy Spirit," which is mentioned in Acts 1:5, and the term, "filled with the Holy Spirit," which we find in Acts 2:4. This, in turn, brings us face to face with the distinction between being sealed by the Holy Spirit and being filled with the Holy Spirit, and what the word *baptism* has to do with each of them. At Pentecost the disciples were filled with the Holy Spirit. Differences of opinion exist as to whether they were sealed and indwelt by the Spirit before Pentecost, or at Pentecost. This much we do know. Whoever is filled with the Spirit of necessity is first sealed and indwelt, whenever salvation takes place.

Paul wrote about "one Lord, one faith, one baptism" (Eph. 4:5). It is interesting, however, that when he wrote about being sealed with the Spirit in Ephesians 1:13, he did not call it baptism. Thus, the question is open whether sealing and indwelling by the Spirit is being baptized into the body.

We must also ask whether Paul had water baptism in mind when he talked about one baptism, or whether this referred to the baptism by, of, with, or in the Holy Spirit. It certainly appears that Paul had water baptism in mind. Justin A. Smith, in his commentary on Ephesians, has this to say about that usage:

> The mention of the "one baptism" in this connection is a striking indication of the significance belonging to this act of Christian obedience. Among all of the many things required, this is selected for express mention. Of the two ordinances enjoined for perpetual observance, this one is named. The reason must be

that while baptism is once for all in a Christian's life, it is that act of obedience in which he binds himself in terms of lasting allegiance to the "one Lord," in a profession of the "one faith". . . . There are not many baptisms, but "one baptism" [*An American Commentary on the New Testament*, ed. Alvah Hovey, vol. 6 (Philadelphia: American Baptist Publishing Society, 1882), p. 61].

The writer here was speaking from the perspective of the Baptist tradition. Thus, he also was saying that it was not only the use of water that was important, but the use of water in a certain way, that is, by immersion. But virtually any commentator who would speak to this issue this way would be saying that water baptism, whether by pouring, sprinkling, or immersion, is "one baptism" and is not repeatable.

Thus, we can say that the Pauline passage of "one Lord, one faith, and one baptism" does not have to do with the baptism of the Holy Spirit. Nor does the Word of God tell us explicitly whether believers are sealed and indwelt by the Holy Spirit as soon as they believe, or when they are baptized with water. If the latter is the case, then those who do not baptize infants could have no hope that infants dying in infancy are saved. And believing adults who are not baptized with water would have no hope. But this specific problem has been discussed by others in detail.

Jesus used the word *baptism* in still another connection, and in that particular usage it had nothing whatever to do either with water or with the Holy Spirit. In Mark 10:38–39 Jesus spoke the following words about baptism:

"You do not know what you ask. Can you drink the cup that I drink, and be baptized with the baptism that I am baptized with?" And they said to Him, "We can." And Jesus said to them, "You will indeed drink the cup that I drink, and with the baptism I am baptized with you will be baptized."

The word *baptism* as used here is a metaphor, having to do with the coming death of the Lord Jesus. It was a strong word indeed. May it not be this word of Jesus to which Paul made reference when he wrote the following?

> Or do you not know that as many of us as were baptized into Christ Jesus were baptized into His death? Therefore we were buried with Him through baptism into death, that just as Christ was raised from the dead by the glory of the Father, even so we also should walk in newness of life (Rom. 6:3–4).

Paul was saying, through the use of a metaphor, the same thing that Jesus was saying. The word *baptism* referred to the death of the Lord Jesus. Yet Paul connected it with water baptism. In any event we do know that the word *baptism* is used in connection with water and with our being born again as well as with what happens to the believer who has received the Holy Spirit.

We must now ask ourselves what Jesus meant when He spoke about the promise of the Father as it relates to the Holy Spirit and to what happened at Pentecost. The word *promise* occurs in Luke 24:49. George R. Bliss, in his commentary on the Gospel of Luke, has this to say·

> The promise means the special influence of the Spirit of God, promised in Joel 2:28. . . . This would be the indispensable prerequisite of the discharge of their (the disciples) office. . . . Not yet fully understanding this, they might be inclined to go forth prematurely [*American Commentary on the New Testament,* vol. 2, p. 353].

Horatio B. Hackett, in his commentary on the Acts of the Apostles, speaks about what the promise of the Father was in the Pentecost event:

> They were all filled with the Holy Spirit . . . a phrase referring usually to special gifts rather than moral qualities, and to these as

transient rather than permanent. (It will be instructive to compare all the other passages in which this expression is found. . . . A study of these passages leads to the conclusion that "being filled with the Holy Spirit," or "being baptized in the Holy Spirit" implies a reception from the Spirit of extraordinary powers, in addition to ordinary sanctifying grace. These extraordinary powers might be permanent, as the gift of prophecy to the apostles, or they might be, and generally were transient, as the gift of miracles) [Ibid., vol. 4, p. 42].

We may conclude, from what these writers have said, that the filling of the Holy Spirit is the baptism of, in, or with the Holy Spirit. They also affirm that the Pentecost event was the fulfillment of the promise of this filling. The disciples were not being sealed and indwelt by the Spirit; they were being filled with the Spirit. They were given gifts by the Spirit, whose power made those gifts viable. This is fully in accord with what we have seen of the operation of the Holy Spirit in the Old Testament. Behind the filling by the Holy Spirit lay the service aspect, by which those who were filled were able to do things they otherwise would have been incapable of doing.

It is also important for us to distinguish between the sanctifying grace of the Holy Spirit, which belongs to all believers and is not something special they must receive, and the filling of the Holy Spirit, which has to do with service. The fruit of the Spirit, of which Paul speaks in Galatians 5:22–23, has to do more with the sanctifying grace of the Holy Spirit than with the impartation of gifts and power for service that come with the infilling of the Holy Spirit.

Another Understanding of Pentecost

Pentecost has been understood in different ways by believers. In fairness, we must review one popular position in our effort to harmonize the data. Two things took place at Pentecost. One of the two is acknowledged by virtually all evangelicals. Pentecost marks the birthday of the church, and the beginning of the church age. It also marked the advent of the Holy Spirit, or what we might properly call the age of the Holy Spirit. Just as the incarnation marked the beginning of the earthly ministry of Jesus, who was at work before this, so Pentecost marks the beginning of the church age ministry of the Spirit who, like Christ, was at work earlier but in a different way. The advent of the church and of the Spirit began at Pentecost.

The second aspect of Pentecost presents a special hermeneutical problem. It revolves around the question whether the believers were sealed and indwelt by the Spirit *before* Pentecost or whether this happened in them for the first time at Pentecost. Many believe that the baptism with the Spirit constituted the sealing and indwelling of all the believers in the upper room when Pentecost came. Others hold that the baptism with the Spirit at Pentecost constituted being filled with the Giver of spiritual gifts and powers for witness for the living of the holy life. How can we resolve this dilemma?

From the data of Scripture in Acts 1 and 2, the following facts are indisputable: (1) Jesus said His disciples would be baptized with the Holy Spirit in a few days' time, and at Pentecost they were so baptized (see Acts 1:5; 2:3). (2) Jesus said that Pentecost was the promise of the Father, and the promise was fulfilled (see Acts 1:4; 2:1–4). (3) All of the disciples were filled with the Holy Spirit. Thus, the baptism with the Spirit, at the very least, includes being filled with the Spirit (see Acts 2:4). (4) The account in Acts says nothing about being sealed and indwelt by the Spirit.

These truths are made known in later Scripture. Paul, in 1 Corinthians 3:16, taught explicitly that the Holy Spirit dwells in every believer. In Ephesians 1:13 Paul wrote that every believer is sealed with the Holy Spirit of promise. In neither case did Paul say whether these things occurred in the hearts of believers at Pentecost or before Pentecost. However, the Ephesians passage speaks of the Holy Spirit of *promise;* and it is conceivable that the use of the word *promise* here specifically refers to Pentecost.

In fairness, let me mention something once again which I alluded to earlier. Since the Scripture is not explicit, it is quite possible that the sealing and the indwelling work of the Spirit did begin at Pentecost. In other words, we can leave the question open to both viewpoints, for it is somewhat academic and does not change the situation for anyone who comes to Jesus Christ for salvation today. At the same time, however, no one can escape that which is explicit; namely, that all the disciples were filled with the Holy Spirit and that this was part of the baptism with the Spirit and the promise of the Father.

The advent of the Spirit and the beginning of the church were first-time and nonrepeatable events. The baptism with the Spirit, however, is a repeatable and necessary act that occurs in whole, and in part, in the lives of all believers. This is true whether we regard the Pentecost event from either of the two perspectives we have just talked about. We can say with certainty that the moment anyone trusts Christ for salvation and is born from above, that new believer is baptized by the Spirit into the body of Christ. And the Holy Spirit takes up His abode in the heart of that believer. When the new birth takes place and the new Christian is sealed and indwelt by the Spirit, is he or she filled with the Spirit? Just as there are conditions that must be met before anyone can be sealed and indwelt, so there are additional conditions that must be met before one can be filled with the Spirit.

Ideally, a new believer should be sealed, indwelt, and filled at the same time. But there are multitudes of believers who have been sealed and indwelt but have not been filled by the Spirit. The reason for this is simple enough. They have not met the conditions for being filled. All of this means that the baptism with the Spirit, in the broadest sense, includes three things—sealing, indwelling, *and* infilling. Thus, whoever is not filled with the Spirit has not received from God all the Scripture included within the term "the baptism with the Spirit."

It would be unwise to say to any believer who has not been filled with the Spirit, "You are a defective or second rate Christian." Rather, the emphasis should be on the fact that God has something for us that is available any time we meet the conditions, which shall be described in more detail in a later chapter. We can assume that in most cases, not being filled with the Spirit does not represent a refusal to take what God has provided, but a lack of adequate understanding, which will be remedied when the truth is properly presented.

We must now ask one further question. What about the external phenomena that were present at Pentecost—the mighty wind, the tongues of fire, and speaking in other languages? Are these to be seen as peculiar only to the Pentecost event, or are they repeatable? For example, in Acts 4, the place was shaken, the disciples were filled again with the Holy Spirit, and they spoke the word of God with boldness. But Luke did not report any speaking in tongues. Other consequences followed, which are never said to have happened again. In Acts 10, when the gift of the Holy Spirit came upon the Gentiles, they spoke in tongues, but that was all.

We will consider shortly whether speaking in other tongues or languages is essential and constitutes the sign of the third aspect of baptism with the Spirit, that is, endowment and enduement for service. This much we know explicitly. When the disciples were filled with the Spirit at Pentecost, it wrought a great transformation in their witness and service, and to this we turn our attention.

SIX

The Holy Spirit in the Early Church

We have seen already that when the Old Testament servants of God were filled with the Holy Spirit, He made a great difference in their lives. Is there evidence to show that the infilling of the Holy Spirit at Pentecost likewise made such a difference?

The most obvious example of what the baptism or filling of the Holy Spirit meant at Pentecost can be seen in the life of Peter. His life is especially instructive, because we know what he was like before Pentecost. Peter, when asked whether he was associated with Jesus, denied his relationship with Him three times. In the final episode of his denials of Jesus, he took an oath in the name of God that he never knew Him. No one could go much further in a denial of the Lord of glory than that. Following the resurrection, Jesus sought out Peter and asked him three times whether he loved Him. This was followed by Jesus' ascension into heaven and the advent of the Holy Spirit.

Did the coming of the Spirit at Pentecost make any difference in Peter's life and witness? Indeed it did. After he was filled with the Holy Spirit, he preached his first apostolic sermon. Even a casual reading of that sermon leads one to conclude that its content went far beyond the ability of that simple fisherman. Moreover, three thousand people responded to the invitation to turn from their sins, believe in Jesus Christ, and be baptized. And these conversions were genuine. For the Word of God says, "They continued steadfastly in the apostles' doctrine and fellowship, in the breaking of bread, and in prayers. Then fear came upon every soul, and many wonders and signs were done through the apostles" (Acts 2:42–43).

From the moment Peter was filled with the Holy Spirit, he became a different man. The Spirit endowed him with the gift of preaching, empowering his words in order to bring men and women to repentance and to faith in Jesus Christ as their Savior.

A short time later when the number of those converted had increased greatly, Peter addressed the high priest and other religious leaders in Jerusalem. The Scripture says he was "filled with the Holy Spirit" (Acts 4:8). When the Jewish scholars "perceived that they [Peter and John] were uneducated and untrained men, they marveled. And they realized that they had been with Jesus" (Acts 4:13). One of the Greek words used in this description is the one from which we get the English word *idiots*. It was the Holy Spirit who gave Peter and John the wisdom and the boldness that confounded their critics.

When the enemies of the faith could not refute the testimony of Peter and John, they set them free. They went back to their fellow believers to report what had happened. When they finished their report, the followers of Jesus began to pray, and "the place where they were assembled together was shaken; and they were all filled with the Holy Spirit, and they spoke the word of God with boldness" (Acts 4:31).

Shortly thereafter, the work of the apostles increased so much they needed help. They arranged for the appointment of seven deacons. The apostles laid down the requirements for the selection of those who might be inducted into this new office. They were to be "men of good reputation, full of the Holy Spirit and wisdom" (Acts 6:3). Among the seven chosen was Stephen, a "man full of faith and the Holy Spirit" (Acts 6:5).

He addressed the high priest and other leading religious leaders, who testified that his face was like the face of an angel (see Acts 6:15). So powerful and moving were his words, that the listeners had only one of two choices: either they had to come to Jesus for salvation, or they had to kill the man who spoke the message. So they stoned Stephen, who became the protomartyr of Christendom. As he died, Stephen said, "Lord Jesus, receive my spirit" (Acts 7:59), and "Lord, do not charge them with this sin" (v. 60).

Subsequent to the stoning of Stephen, the people of the Way were persecuted and brought before the courts. In fact, one of those who stood by and watched Stephen die was a man named Saul (see Acts 8:1). He was a Pharisee who hated Jesus and the people who followed Him. Saul carried letters on the road to Damascus that would enable him to capture any of the people of the Way in that city (see Acts 9). Enroute to Damascus, Jesus interrupted his journey and brought him to salvation. Blinded, Saul had to be led to Damascus to the house of Judas on the street called Straight. God commanded Ananias to put his hands on Saul so that he would receive his sight and be filled with the Holy Spirit. The Scripture says, "Immediately he preached Christ in the synagogues, that He is the Son of God" (Acts 9:20).

This man Saul was taught and led by the Holy Spirit. Best of all, he was filled with the Holy Spirit. This was true of him all the days of his life. He enjoyed what we might call a steady state.

It was Saul, whom we call Paul, who later wrote the book of Ephesians. In that book he said, "And do not be drunk with wine, in which is dissipation; but be filled with the Spirit" (Eph. 5:18). From this verse we learn several valuable lessons. The first is that not all believers are filled with the Spirit. The second is that believers ought to be filled with the Spirit. The third is that God never commands us to do what it is impossible

97

for us to do. Thus, a Spirit-filled life is the birthright, a part of the inheritance of every child of God. No one can keep any believer from being filled with the Spirit except the believer himself or herself.

Pentecost, then, introduced the new age of the Spirit. It opened a door of blessing to all believers. God provided a foretaste of what that meant by showing us what being filled with the Spirit meant to so many of His servants in the Old Testament. Unfortunately, many of today's books about the Holy Spirit have highlighted the experience of the Spirit's filling by centering their attention on evangelists, ministers, and other highly placed leaders in the churches of Jesus Christ. This leaves the impression that the filling of the Spirit is only for the few and mighty—not for the everyday believer. This was true, to a degree, in the Old Testament, but not the New. The Spirit's filling is available to the housewife, the businessman, the truck driver, the secretary, the physician, the college student, and the men and women on the assembly lines of the factories. One does not have to be a specially-called servant of God to qualify. No one is excluded from this blessing, and every life can be a better one when it is lived in the power of the Holy Spirit.

Pentecost and Glossolalia

At Pentecost and in this generation, much emphasis has been placed on the signs that accompany the filling or baptism with the Spirit. This emphasis seems to dwell especially on *glossolalia* or speaking in tongues. Tongues speaking has aroused a great deal of controversy and has produced strong statements both for and against it. Of one thing there can be no doubt: glossolalia was manifested at Pentecost and is mentioned in several other places in the Acts of the Apostles (see

10:46; 19:6). Paul dealt with the gift of tongues in 1 Corinthians 12–14, where he admitted to the blessing in his own life.

At its roots, the difference of opinion depends on how one answers the question whether the baptism with the Spirit must include, for its inward witness to the believers, speaking in some kind of a tongue. We have already mentioned that the Assemblies of God denomination, for example, is committed to tongues as *the* sign of the baptism. Many of those in the dispensational tradition believe that the gift of tongues ceased at the end of the apostolic period and is not for this present age. Some in this tradition have gone so far as to say that speaking in tongues is demonic.

Most people would allege that the experience of speaking in tongues is not usually that of speaking known languages. Support for this has come from some language scholars who have investigated the speech of those whose words in tongues have been recorded. They assert that the sounds of those who speak in tongues lack certain ingredients common to all known languages.

At Pentecost the disciples of Jesus spoke in known, earthly languages. Today, however, tongues speakers say that the languages are Holy Spirit utterances that are not to be equated with known languages. They may be the tongues of angels, such as those mentioned by Paul in 1 Corinthians 13:1, and, as such, may not be identical with known human languages. People who endorse speaking in tongues not infrequently refer to them as ecstatic utterances, "Spirit-talk," or prayer language.

The situation would be ameliorated considerably if pentecostal believers spoke of tongues as *a* sign of the filling, rather than *the* sign of the filling. This would leave the door open for the Spirit to manifest Himself to believers in other ways, or in no particular way. We do know that no one in the Old Testament, on whom the Spirit came, is said to have spoken in tongues. Jesus never spoke in tongues nor did John the Baptist, Elizabeth, Zacharias, or Mary. And Joel's prophecy certainly seems to locate the phenomenon at and after Pentecost.

In the days following the Reformation, many people who received the infilling baptism with the Spirit, and who used that term in describing it, had no tongues experience. Finney, Moody, and Torrey never spoke in tongues. Yet all of these did have an inner experience connected with their filling or baptism. If speaking in tongues is a necessary accompaniment of the baptism with the Spirit, then one would have to say that Moody, Finney, and Torrey were wrong in supposing they had such an experience. C. I. Scofield, of the Scofield Bible, is still remembered as one of the foremost promotors of dispensational theology. It is illuminating that when he spoke at the funeral of D. L. Moody, he said that Moody had received the baptism with the Spirit. This term, however, is not popular among most dispensationalists today.

Among some pentecostals, who are eager and anxious for all to enjoy what they have experienced, there is a tendency to intimate that those who have not spoken in tongues are inferior Christians. In addition, some go even further and intimate by the way they act that speaking in tongues is the goal rather than a sign of something more essential, that is, the fullness of the Spirit. There are at least a few who identify themselves as pentecostals who suppose that speaking in tongues makes a discussion of theology immaterial. To them, what you believe makes little difference so long as you have spoken in tongues—a dangerous viewpoint, if for no other reason than that the devil himself can counterfeit tongues.

Throughout history, numbers of non-Christian peoples have spoken in tongues. Can tongues, then, be genuine, when the theology is clearly defective? We must also assert as forcefully as we can that our attention should be fixed on the truth before the experience, on the Giver more than the gift. Speaking in tongues must never supplant the Person of the Holy Spirit and the promises of the Holy Scripture.

When we speak about the signs that accompany the filling or baptism with the Spirit, we must remember that signs can be inward or outward. The outward signs may vary, for the Spirit cannot be boxed in to any single sign (unless the Scriptures so indicate, and they do not do so explicitly). There is one inward sign we ought never to ignore. That is the sign of our faith. We can and should believe that we are filled with the Holy Spirit, when we have met the conditions, whether there is an outward sign of an experiential sort or not. We do not need an experiential sign, either for salvation or for the Spirit's baptism, in order to have what we all want. When we talk about any outward sign of the filling, we should not forget the inward sign.

The fullness of the Spirit, as we have said, is intended to impart to us a gift or gifts of the Spirit—that is, an endowment—and the enduement of the Spirit—that is, the power we need to make the fullest use of the gift or gifts we have been given. The power is more important for its outward effect than any inner sign. If I have the gift of being an evangelist, it will be manifested outwardly by the fact that many more people will come to a saving knowledge of Jesus Christ than did so before I had the filling.

King Saul was given the gift of prophecy and so he prophesied. So did Elijah and Elisha. So did Jeremiah, Ezekiel, Isaiah, and all of the authors of Scripture. They were filled with the Spirit, and it was under the Spirit's tutelage that they wrote the Word of God. All of the miracles performed by Moses, Elijah, Elisha, and apostles, and even the Lord Jesus Christ came about through the power of the Holy Spirit. In the case of Jesus, He had the power in Himself to perform miracles since He was very God of very God. But as true man, He was filled with the Holy Spirit and, as a man, had the Spirit's power. This is a great mystery to be sure.

The Pentecost event was never designed to produce a sense of pride in anyone filled with the Holy Spirit. Nor was it intended to grade Christians as good, better, and best. You and I are not better than other people because we have been saved. And we cannot approach an unbeliever as though we were superior to him or her. We have nothing whatever about which to boast. We have been saved by grace through faith, and even faith is the gift of God.

So also with the infilling of the Spirit. This, too, springs from the grace of God. If and when we speak of it, we must do so with humility. The incoming of pride in enjoying what is a gift is one of the surest ways to quench the Spirit, as we shall see in greater detail later.

The Gifts of the Holy Spirit

Pentecost marked the beginning of the church age. Thus it was an epochal event in the history of redemption and in the progressive unfolding of the revelation of God. The Old Testament was given to us, beginning with Moses and the Pentateuch and ending with the Book of Malachi. This marked the closing of the Old Testament canon of Scripture.

Then followed what historians call the four hundred silent years. During this period of time nothing more was added to the written revelation of God. None of the New Testament was written until after Pentecost. Then, in a period of a little more than half a century, all of the New Testament was recorded for us. At the close of the first century, the written revelation of God came to a close. This means that for almost two thousand years since the closing of the New Testament canon, nothing has been added to the written Word of God. And nothing more will be added.

From this vantage point we may say that just as there were four hundred silent years between the Old and the New Testaments, so there have been almost two thousand years of silence (so far as new revelation is concerned) since the New Testament was completed. But the beginning of the church age marked the beginning of the age of the Holy Spirit in a special way. And the Holy Spirit is constantly doing His work in this age.

So far as the church is concerned, it is the function of the Holy Spirit to equip the people of God for ministry. This equipping of the people of God is one of the vital elements that made up the Pentecost event. Since then, the Holy Spirit has been at work to endow and endue the people of God for the ongoing life of the church and its ministry. In doing this work, the Holy Spirit gives both gifts and power to the people of God for service in the church, which is the body of Christ. Every believer should understand that the Holy Spirit has some spiritual gift for him or for her. And these gifts are made usable by the Spirit's power. Thus, the baptism of the Spirit or the infilling of the Spirit is not, and should not, be thought of primarily as an experience. Nor is it something given for the personal benefit of any individual. It has to do with the glory of God and the ongoing life of the church.

In Scripture, the church is pictured as the body of Christ. This figure is used again and again, with emphasis on the different parts of the human body. Some parts of the body are of less usefulness than other parts, but no part is without worth. If anyone has lost a finger, a leg, an eye, or a hand or foot, that person, and anyone who looks at that person, realizes that he or she is handicapped. The church is an organism that resembles the human body. It is constituted of many parts. If any part is missing, the body is incomplete. Therefore, the Holy Spirit gives diverse gifts to all members of the body and the power to use those gifts for the ministry of the churches. Everybody has some special gift that, when that person is filled with the Holy Spirit, is heightened and made powerful for service to God.

Peter Wagner, to whom I am deeply indebted for the material that follows, has said, "A spiritual gift is a special attribute given by the Holy Spirit to every member of the body of Christ according to God's grace for use within the context of the body." What are these spiritual gifts, and which one, or ones, do you and I have?

The list of the gifts will vary in number. I will add a few to the twenty-seven Peter Wagner has suggested. We need not suppose that any one list is the last word that may be spoken on this subject. Paul the apostle is the one who tells us more particularly what the gifts of the Spirit are. He does so in Romans 12, 1 Corinthians 12, and Ephesians 4. Most commentators agree that the list of gifts in these passages of Scripture number twenty. Others have been added by different people who have written on the subject.

1. *Prophecy.* A gift given to a limited number of God's people, prophecy consists in the special ability to receive and to communicate an immediate message of God to His people through a divinely anointed utterance. This gift includes foretelling and forthtelling. Foretelling has to do with uttering prophecies of what will happen in the future, while forthtelling involves understanding and being able to proclaim the Word of God knowledgeably through preaching. Today there can be no new revelation that can be regarded as an addition to the Bible. But God can make known, through the prophetic gift, what is His will, or what He is about to do.

2. *Service.* This gift involves a special ability to recognize unmet needs and to make use of available resources to meet

those needs and to help accomplish desired goals within the church.

3. *Teaching.* God enables the teacher to communicate information related to the health and ministry of the body and its members in such a manner that others will learn.

4. *Exhortation.* This gift equips one to minister words of comfort, consolation, encouragement, and counsel to those who feel the need to be helped and healed. It also includes the ability to bring people to a point of decision for salvation.

5. *Giving.* A person with the gift of giving is enabled to contribute beyond the tithe material resources to the work of God with liberality and cheerfulness.

6. *Leadership.* This is the ability to communicate goals to others in such a way that they will voluntarily and harmoniously work together to accomplish those goals for the glory of God and the advancement of His kingdom.

7. *Mercy.* The ability to feel genuine empathy and compassion for believers and unbelievers who suffer distressing physical, mental, or emotional problems comes with the gift of mercy. This gift allows its recipient to translate that compassion into cheerfully executed works or deeds that reflect the love of Jesus Christ and alleviate suffering.

8. *Wisdom.* This is the gift of knowing the mind of the Spirit in such a way as to have insight as to how given knowledge may best be applied to specific needs arising in the body of Christ. Deacons, for example, are required to have the gift of wisdom in dealing with the material needs and everyday matters of a local church.

9. *Knowledge.* The ability to uncover, accumulate, analyze, and clarify ideas and information are important and necessary to the growth and well-being of the body of Christ.

10. *Faith.* The gift of faith equips a believer to discern, with extraordinary confidence, what the will of God is, and to know

that God will do what is asked of Him. The *grace* of faith, given to all believers, means they can have faith to receive whatever is specifically promised to all by God. The *gift* of faith rests on no explicit promise of God but on the Spirit's revelation that what is desired is indeed the will of God and, thus, is guaranteed to come to pass.

11. *Healing.* This is the special ability given to someone who serves as a human intermediary, through whom it pleases God to cure illness and restore health, apart from the use of natural means.

12. *Miracles.* A special ability is given to some to be intermediaries through whom it pleases God to perform powerful acts that are perceived by observers to have altered the ordinary course of nature.

13. *Discerning Spirits.* By this gift, the recipient is able to know with assurance whether certain behavior or events, purported to be of God, are in reality divine, or only human, or satanic.

14. *Tongues.* This is the gift whereby the recipient speaks to God in a language he has never known or learned, and/or the reception and communication of an immediate message from God to His people through a divinely given utterance.

15. *Interpretation.* The special ability given to some to make known to others, in the common vernacular, the content of a message given by one who speaks in tongues.

16. *Apostle.* This is the ability to assume and exercise general leadership over a number of churches, with an extraordinary authority in spiritual matters. This gift is spontaneously recognized and appreciated by those churches. In the early church, both the gifts of prophecy and apostleship were seen as being incorporated into the office of bishop.

17. *Helps.* The recipient of this gift is able to invest his talents in the life and ministry of other members of the body in

order to enable them to increase the effectiveness of their own spiritual gifts.

18. *Administration.* This gift enables the recipient to understand clearly the immediate and long range goals of a particular unit of the body of Christ and to devise and execute plans for the effective accomplishment of those goals.

19. *Evangelist.* This constitutes the ability of sharing the gospel in such a way that large numbers of men and women become disciples of Jesus Christ and responsible members of a church. All believers are to do the work of evangelism, but the gift of an evangelist produces an enlarged harvest.

20. *Pastor.* The recipient is able to assume a long-term personal responsibility for the spiritual welfare of a small or large group of believers.

21. *Celibacy.* This gift enables one to remain single without suffering undue sexual temptations and is accompanied by conscientious devotion to the Lord.

22. *Voluntary Poverty.* This gift enables the recipient to renounce material comfort and luxury and to adopt a personal lifestyle comparable to those living at the poverty level in a given society, doing this in order to serve God more effectively. Both poverty and celibacy, of course, have been central to monastic life throughout history.

23. *Martyrdom.* The recipient of this gift is enabled to undergo suffering for the faith, even unto death, while consistently displaying a joyous and victorious attitude that brings great glory to God.

24. *Hospitality.* The recipient of this gift is able to provide an open house, warm welcome, and happy fellowship for those in need of food and lodging.

25. *Missionary.* This gift enables one to minister to those of another culture using whatever spiritual gifts he or she may have.

26. *Intercession.* An intercessor is enabled to pray for extended periods of time on a regular basis, and to see frequent and specific answers to prayer, to a degree much greater than that which is common to the average believer.

27. *Exorcism.* This constitutes the ability to cast out demons and evil spirits.

28. *Music.* A musician may be specially gifted to enhance the worship of God and to meet the needs of believers through the use of singing and instrumental music.

29. *Writing.* Through this gift, the recipient can make known to believers and unbelievers, through the written word, the excellencies of the mind of God.

30. *Craftsmanship.* This is the gift whereby the recipient can make objects of lasting beauty in the form of art, painting, and sculpture, for the glory of God. Bezaleel, in Exodus 31:3, is an illustration of one so gifted by the Holy Spirit.

Today there are Christians who do not perceive that they have spiritual gifts, or if they think they are gifted in some way, they use their gifts in the energy of the flesh. Some believers have gifts in inchoate form, that is, they are imperfectly formed and wait for the quickening power of the Holy Spirit to bring the gift or gifts to maturity. Like buds on a rose bush, they need to be opened to full flower. And the gifts are of limited value if they are not accompanied by the power of the Holy Spirit.

The giving of the Holy Spirit at Pentecost opened the flood gates, of which Jesus spoke when He said that rivers of living water would flow from His people. It remains only for the people of God to receive the gift of the Holy Spirit, which is nothing less than the filling or baptism with the Spirit.

SEVEN

The Filling of the Holy Spirit

A Review of the Background

We have learned that the revelation of God is progressive. The Bible did not end with the closing of the thirty-nine books of the Old Testament canon. God graciously continued to reveal more about Himself and to make known to us truths that either were hidden in the Old Testament or have now been revealed to us in ways previously unknown. The Holy Spirit, as we have seen, was operative in the Old Testament, but new aspects of His work have been made known to us in the New Testament.

In the Old Testament, the Holy Spirit came upon chosen vessels of God at His pleasure. He gave those people gifts and power. When this happened, the recipients were able to do what they had been incapable of doing before they were gifted in this way. At the heart of the Spirit's working was the accomplishment of the divine purpose of God for the world and for the salvation of men and women. But there is nothing in the Old Testament that leads us to suppose that the Spirit's special power was available to all (except for that which came through the common grace of God). The New Testament, however, brings to the fore something that is both old and startlingly new.

Beginning at Pentecost, the Father and the Son sent the

Holy Spirit to be the divine witness to the Son of God, who had ascended into heaven and is now seated at the right hand of God the Father. One of the Spirit's works is to convict unbelievers of sin and to regenerate them through their faith in Jesus Christ.

The Holy Spirit does two things immediately in the hearts and lives of sinners who, through faith in Jesus, are justified and regenerated. First, He *seals* every new believer. Paul spoke of this work of the Holy Spirit in Ephesians 1:13–14:

> In Him you also trusted, after you heard the word of truth, the gospel of your salvation; in whom also, having believed, you were sealed with the Holy Spirit of promise, who is the guarantee of our inheritance until the redemption of the purchased possession, to the praise of His glory.

When we have been baptized by the Spirit into the body of Christ, we are not only sealed—that is, marked off as God's possession until the day of final redemption at the end of the age—we are also, secondly, *indwelt* by the Holy Spirit. He takes up his abode in our hearts. In 1 Corinthians 3:16 Paul wrote that we are "the temple of God," and that "the Spirit of God dwells in [us]." In 2 Corinthians 1:22 Paul wrote the same thing: "[God] also has sealed us and given us the Spirit in our hearts as a deposit."

The sealing and the indwelling of the Holy Spirit occurs in the lives of all believers as soon as they are born again. He does these things whether they know it or feel it. (Of course, all believers can and should know this reality from the Scriptures and accept it as true, whether there is any subjective experience or apprehension of these truths or not.) The same Holy Spirit is also engaged in the work of sanctification, by which He conforms believers to the image or likeness of Jesus Christ. Sanctification and holiness belong together, for the end of sanctification is a life of holiness. Holiness—being set apart unto God—connotes the presence of righteousness; right thoughts and right conduct. Negatively, holiness implies the absence of sin. At all times, the Holy Spirit is at work in all believers' lives, applying sanctifying grace through which Christian people become more and more like Jesus Christ.

We see then, that all believers are sealed, indwelt, and experience the sanctifying grace of the Spirit in them. But not every believer is, at the time of the new birth or even later, necessarily filled or controlled by the Holy Spirit. The filling of which we speak is certainly the believer's birthright. It belongs to him or her because he or she is a child of God and a joint heir with Jesus Christ. It is the Father's wish that all of His children be filled with the Spirit. It is a blessing that must be claimed.

In the Old Testament, male babies were circumcised. This was a sign of the covenant, and thus the infant was counted among the people of God. When that child reached his thirteenth birthday, he was regarded as coming into adulthood and celebrated his coming of age in a ceremony called the bar mitzvah. It was then that he assumed his religious duty and responsibility. He confirmed the covenant, of which circumcision was the sign, and identified himself with the people of God.

Luke assumed this tradition when he wrote of Jesus' coming to the temple when He was twelve. He went with His parents to the Passover feast, which all males were required to attend at Jerusalem. He openly identified Himself with the people of God and confirmed the covenant when He asked and answered questions of doctors of the Law at the temple. They were astounded "at His understanding and answers" (Luke 2:47).

Is it not in similar vein that we who have been redeemed are to claim the filling of the Holy Spirit, which belongs to us by the new birth and covenant promise but comes to us only when we appropriate the promise that God has given to us?

The Loss of the Spirit's Filling
and the Possible Loss of Salvation

Let us underscore, at this point, one item of theology about which the people of God have entertained differing views for four hundred years. There are Arminians, who think that a true believer can lose his salvation or fall from grace. On the other hand, Calvinists insist that once a person is saved, that person will persevere by the work of the Spirit; that is, he or she will never fall from grace. The point at issue is important, because we shall see that those who have been filled with the Holy Spirit may lose that blessing and regain it once again. But this is quite different from saying that a believer can lose the sealing and the indwelling of the Holy Spirit and be thrust back into an unregenerate state. Backsliding, of course, is always a possibility, but it presumes that the backslider can and will return to the right relationship he had with God when he first believed.

The question must be posed—if it is possible for a true believer to lose his salvation and be cut off from the people of God, will he ever be able to return again to a state of grace? In other words, can he be "born again" more than once? The Scriptures certainly specify, as we shall see in detail, how a believer can lose the filling of the Holy Spirit. But nowhere in the Word of God is it stated that one who hypothetically has fallen from grace can be saved a second time. Christ was crucified once for the sins of men. He would have to be crucified a second time, and this is an impossibility. Hebrews 6:4–6 answers the question decisively:

> For it is impossible for those who were once enlightened, and have tasted the heavenly gift, and have become partakers of the Holy Spirit, and have tasted the good word of God and the powers of the age to come, if they fall away, to renew them again to repentance, since they crucify again for themselves the Son of God, and put Him to an open shame.

Surely we can leave open the question whether a regenerated person can fall from grace. But we must insist that, if it is possible, then that one can never return to a state of grace and is lost forever. However, one can be filled with the Spirit and lose that blessing without losing his or her salvation. And the same believer who has lost this blessing can regain it by the grace of God. So we come now to answer the question how believers who have been sealed and indwelt by the Spirit may also be filled with the Holy Spirit.

1. The Necessity for the New Birth

The first requirement for our being filled with the Spirit is to be born of God through union with Jesus Christ. No one can be filled with the Spirit who has not believed.

Did this same principle apply to the saints of the Old Testament? Surely Moses, Elijah, Elisha, and all the prophets who were filled with the Spirit were saints of God. Everyone in the Old Testament who was saved, responded to God the same way Abraham did—by faith. They looked forward to Calvary even as we look backward to it. Calvary is the focal point of salvation history for both the Old and New Testament saints. We can say firmly that the Holy Spirit filled only God's people in the Old Testament, but the filling was by the choice of the Spirit and it was not available to any and all saints who wanted it. Today, the Holy Spirit is available to any and all true believers.

And consider this rich promise of Christ:

> "But you do not believe, because you are not of My sheep, as I said to you. My sheep hear My voice, and I know them, and they follow Me. And I give them eternal life, and they shall never perish; neither shall anyone snatch them out of My hand. My Father, who has given them to Me, is greater than all; and no one is able to snatch them out of My Father's hand" (John 10:26–29)

Pentecost had not yet come Jesus was talking to His temple

listeners about those who were His sheep right then and there. They were, if you please, still "Old Testament people." And to them He gave the offer of eternal life. He also implied that those who refused to believe on Him were outside the kingdom of God (see v. 26). From the New Testament account of those who were saved in Jesus' day before Pentecost, we can read back into the Old Testament the fact that it was the same Holy Spirit who brought conviction of sin and righteousness and judgment. So the fact that the Holy Spirit was at work in the Old Testament is stated with clarity in the New Testament.

In these latter days, the revelation of God is explicit that only those can be filled with the Holy Spirit who have been regenerated and thus sealed and indwelt by the Spirit. The unregenerate person is dead in trespasses and sins. He or she is not, will not be, and cannot be interested in the filling of the Holy Spirit. It makes no sense to the unconverted mind. Conversion, however, is no guarantee that the new person in Christ will be interested in being filled with the Spirit immediately or consistently. All the new birth guarantees is that the believer may think like a Christian and have everything available to him or her that he or she needs to live a Christian life. Whereas he or she formerly could not think like a Christian, by reason of the new birth he or she now may think rightly. It is only through the reading of the Word of God or the faithful preaching of that Word, that the believer comes to know and to think rightly about the infilling of the Holy Spirit.

The sad fact is that many Christians do not read the Word of God. They remain ignorant of the promise of God to fill them with His Spirit. And the pulpits of the land rarely expound this teaching adequately. People in the charismatic movement, and those in the pentecostal tradition, as well as Wesleyans who emphasize the second blessing—whether we agree theologically with them or not—have drawn our attention to the person and work of the Holy Spirit. They have persistently reminded the rest of us that there are some wonderful things in store for believers subsequent to regeneration. The filling of the Spirit and personal holiness are dynamically related, but the differences of nomenclature have often proved to be a stumbling block to many who lack enthusiasm for the use of such terms as the second baptism, a second work of grace, perfectionism, and the *necessity* for a glossolalic experience (speaking in tongues).

If the new birth is the first prerequisite for being filled with the Spirit, the second one has to do with the lordship of Jesus Christ.

2. The Necessity of Being Under the Lordship of Christ

The Scriptures affirm that Jesus Christ is both Savior and Lord. That is true even when it may not be appropriated in personal experience. Most people who are converted understand the meaning of the saviorhood of Jesus. They know that through repentance toward God the Father and faith in the Lord Jesus Christ they are saved from judgment for their sins. They also talk about Jesus as Lord, but for them the term often means something quite different from what is described in the Scriptures. What does the lordship of Christ mean from the biblical perspective?

In Romans 1:3 Paul wrote about "Jesus Christ our Lord." But in the opening of the book, Paul identified himself as "a servant of Christ Jesus." It is the word *servant* that holds the key to the question of Christ's lordship.

When we think of the word *servant* today, we have in mind something that is far different from the meaning of the word in Paul's day. He used the Greek word *doulos*, which meant "slave." The term in his day had legal implications, in which a distinction was made between a hired servant who had rights and privileges, and a slave who had none. The owner of the slave had the right of life and death over the one who was in bondage to him. The master could kill his slave for any reason and could do so with impunity. In the strictest sense of the term, the master owned the slave, body and soul.

When Paul used the term, then, he meant that he was owned and controlled by Jesus Christ, who had the right of life and death over him. He was no mere servant of Jesus. He was His slave and was at his Master's disposal, to do whatever He commanded him to do. He had no right to ask any questions, and he could not counter any command with other alternatives. He was, in the truest sense of the term, under the lordship of Christ.

Before anyone can be filled with the Holy Spirit, he or she must voluntarily come under the lordship of Jesus Christ in the sense of being a slave. This choice will not be forced on anyone, but it is the second condition set down for those who wish to be filled with the Holy Spirit.

We need to remember that Adam was given the freedom to choose in the Garden of Eden. This freedom made him a responsible agent. We who are in Christ have received in principle all that we lost through Adam in Eden. Conversion brings us into a position where we have the freedom to assume the role of bondslave (or servant), but we do not have to do so. When we fail to make Jesus Christ Lord in this way, we cannot claim the promise of God to give us what we need to live life on the highest plane. The norm for Christian life is to have Christ sitting on the throne of our hearts. Paradoxically, when Christ is truly Lord, this is when the believer reaches the highest point of self-fulfillment.

In a sense, Christ is not Lord *at* all if He is not Lord *of* all. One's commitment to the lordship of Christ is a one-time commitment that should be regarded as an irrevocable and irreversible decision. It is possible that the application of His lordship to daily life may be imperfect at times, but the intention should be there to do His will. If at any time the believer who has been Spirit-filled does not let Jesus have His way and will, he or she will quench the power of the Holy Spirit, destroy fellowship with Jesus, and be in need of immediate repentance and forgiveness.

It is important to note again that the acceptance of the lordship of Christ is a necessary prerequisite to being filled with the Holy Spirit. No one can be Spirit-filled without first coming under the reign of Christ.

When speaking about the lordship of Christ, we should always do so within the larger context of the church. Jesus Christ is the Lord of the church even as He is Lord of each of its members. The church is His body, and each believer is a member of that one body. We can speak of the church as comprising all believers of all ages, past, present, and future. This invisible church, which is known only to God, is empirically manifested in visible churches. It is through the visible churches that God, through the Spirit, does His work.

When we speak of being filled with the Spirit, we must assert the central role of the church, which is Christ's body. Normally, the infilling of the Holy Spirit should occur within the worshiping and preaching ministry of the local congregation. If it takes place apart from the worshiping community, it must still be seen within the context of the church, because the filled one is part of the body, and the body is the church. There is no such thing as solitary Christianity. We are indivisibly united with believers who are in heaven, those who are alive on earth, and those who are yet unborn but will become part of Christ's church.

If there is anything the lordship of Christ does, it is to bring us closer together as fellow members of the body, which is the church, so that all of life is lived within that context.

3. Confession and Repentance

The third step in securing the fullness of the Holy Spirit has to do with the cleansing of the vessel the Holy Spirit is about to fill. He does not come into a dirty vessel or sit on the throne of a heart that has been defiled by sin. The believer who wishes to be filled with the Spirit must take a close look at his or her life and ask the Spirit to show him or her what he or she needs to confess. Every known sin must be dealt with. There is no need to worry about sins one cannot remember; it is enough to take care of the sins we do know about. If there are still other unknown sins, the Holy Spirit, at His good pleasure, will bring them to mind and they can then be dealt with.

The two components of this third requirement for living the Spirit-filled life are repentance and confession. Confession, in and of itself, is not sufficient. The believer must be sorry for his or her sins. Those sins must be forsaken. He or she must turn to Jesus Christ for cleansing. Then it is that he or she should make confession to God, who has provided the remedy for transgressions.

In 1 John 1:9 the Scripture says, "If we confess our sins, He is faithful and just to forgive us our sins and to cleanse us from all unrighteousness." The promise is made by God that every sin that is confessed will be forgiven, and our hearts will be cleansed from all unrighteousness. The moment our sins are confessed and Christ is Lord, we stand blameless before the Lord God. At that moment, we are holy in God's sight. And we remain holy until such time that we sin, which then requires repentance, confession, cleansing, and restoration to a position of blamelessness before the Lord God.

God unconditionally promises the forgiveness of sins when we repent and confess. When believers have been made pure by repentance and confession, the third indispensable condition for obtaining the Holy Spirit's fullness has been met. What remains for us to do?

4. Asking God to Fill Us with His Holy Spirit

We cannot suppose that the fullness of the Holy Spirit will come in other ways than is outlined for us in the Word of God. When the Holy Spirit came at Pentecost and the believers were filled, they had waited for ten days. Acts 1:14 reads, "These all continued with one accord in prayer and supplication, with the women and Mary the mother of Jesus, and with His brothers." Jesus had promised them that the Spirit would come. They waited. And while they waited, they prayed for what Jesus had promised them. They believed Him and were expectantly looking for the Spirit. It is very important for us to note one or two things about this ten-day waiting period.

Since Pentecost had not yet come and the old dispensation was still in force, the Spirit came and went at his own sovereign pleasure. The Holy Spirit had come upon the mother of Jesus when she conceived Him. Moreover, Elizabeth and Zacharias were both filled with the Holy Spirit. In addition, we read in John 20:22 that Jesus breathed on the disciples and said, "Receive the Holy Spirit." Surely those who had been filled with the Holy Spirit would not have been waiting for something they already had. The new age was about to dawn. The Holy Spirit, who had come and gone as He pleased, was about to come and abide forever. They, who had experienced the Spirit's fullness for a period of time, were to be able to have the Spirit's fullness for all time as they met the conditions described in Scripture.

Undoubtedly the Holy Spirit brought back to their minds what Jesus had said: "How much more will your heavenly Father give the Holy Spirit to those who ask Him!" (Luke 11:13). The other conditions having been fulfilled, it would be foolish not to ask God to give what He had promised.

At this point, before speaking of the fifth condition laid down to secure the Spirit's fullness, a word should be said about the believer's attitude toward the infilling of which we are speak-

119

ing. This may be summarized by six statements: (1) The Spirit's fullness is the Christian's birthright. It belongs to him or her by way of promise in the covenant of redemption. (2) The promise of the Spirit was made available to all believers once Pentecost had come. (3) Every believer knows whether he or she has the Spirit's fullness. If one does not know one has the Spirit's fullness, then one does not have it. (4) The Scripture makes it evident that no one can secure the fullness of the Spirit by one's own efforts. Nor can it be bought, as is made clear by the example of Simon the Sorcerer (see Acts 8:9–25). (5) Every sincere believer should obtain the Spirit's fullness, whatever the price may be. (6) The believer can be certain that if he or she meets the conditions set down for receiving the fullness of the Holy Spirit, he or she is sure to receive it, because God always keeps His word.

5. Claiming the Promise

The believer who asks God to fill him or her with His Holy Spirit should do so with certain biblical facts in mind and heart. The first is that it is the will of God for each believer to be filled with the Spirit. If this is so, then it is something that can be prayed for without contingency, because whatever is the will of God can be asked for with the certitude of faith. The apostle John put it this way: "Now this is the confidence that we have in Him, that if we ask anything according to His will, He hears us. And if we know that He hears us, whatever we ask, we know that we have the petitions that we have asked of Him" (1 John 5:14–15). This means that the believer can pray this prayer for the Spirit's fullness in faith, believing that the request will be granted.

This marks the difference between the grace of faith and the gift of faith. The gift of faith may come to the believer by the Holy Spirit when prayer is offered for something for which there is no explicit promise from the Word of God. But when there is an explicit promise, there the grace of faith reigns. The grace of faith means we can trust God for the matter, because He has already promised that He will do it because it is His will. If we do not believe what God has promised, this is sin, which needs to be repented of and confessed.

Every believer who serves Christ as Lord, who has repented of and confessed all known sin, and who has asked to be filled with the Holy Spirit can claim the promise of God in faith. It is here that the dragon of delay—the agonizing and waiting breathlessly for the fulfillment of the divine promise—is unnecessary. Nor should the anticipation be based upon looking for or demanding some outward sign. Nowhere does Scripture say that there is only one sign or confirmation marking the Spirit's fullness. The Promise of God is kept even when there may be no sign at all. We are not to look for an experience. We are simply to accept the promise by faith, and begin to thank God for what He has already done.

It would be wrong to claim that there will necessarily be *no* external or inward corroborating evidence by which the infilling of the Holy Spirit may be discerned experientially. Just as the experiences of those who are converted differ widely, so will the experiences of those who are filled with the Spirit vary from person to person. Upon conversion, some experience a great sense of relief. Some laugh for joy. Others cry. Some feel nothing. Others have a peace they never had known before. The certainty of conversion derives, not from any experience, but from the living and true Word of God.

How do I know I am saved? I know because the Word of God says so. Jesus said, "He who hears My word and believes in Him who sent Me has everlasting life, and shall not come into judgment, but has passed from death into life" (John 5:24). Once the conditions for salvation have been fulfilled, the Word of God gives to those who so believe the certainty their hearts crave—whether there is any experience or not. The same thing is true with regard to the infilling of the Holy Spirit. Having met the conditions, on the authority of the Word of God, the believer can say in simple faith that he or she now is filled with the Holy Spirit.

Some people think it is necessary to wait for some time after asking for the filling of the Holy Spirit before it takes place. It is true that this has been the experience of a number of believers who have agonized and waited because they were not properly instructed. They thought the infilling would take place only if they spent a long time in prayer, begging God and anguishing. In virtually every instance of this sort the petitioner was looking for some sign of the filling, some great light, or a swelling tide of power that increased in intensity. These are not needed, nor do they have to be experienced before the filling takes place. Faith lays hold of the promise of God, embraces that promise, and believes that the answer has come, whether or not there is any outward, visible sign. All we need to do is to thank God, receive, and accept the filling as an accomplished fact. External corroborating evidence may come later.

EIGHT
Examples of Spirit-Filled Believers

Let us suppose for a moment that a believer is filled with the Holy Spirit. Does it make a difference in his or her life? Of what value is being filled with the Spirit, if nothing happens to the infilled believer, or if there is no change in his or her life and ministry?

It is to the glory of the Father that He sent Jesus Christ, His Son, to do more than tell us what we should be like. Almost anyone can lay down ideal standards of what people should be as Christians. But who can show us, by the way he or she lives, that the standards that are laid down are attainable? The wonder of Jesus is that He not only called us to a certain kind of life. He Himself lived the kind of life He commanded others to live. He was the living example of what the ideal Spirit-filled person would be like.

Jesus was God and man. He was the perfect man and the infinite God. Those of us who follow Him will find our ultimate perfection when glorification occurs immediately upon death. But what we ought to be can be observed in some distinctive and clearly manifested fashion, in the lives of those who follow the Son of God. To reach this stature of the fullness of Christ in this life, every believer needs a power that does not reside in human beings. This is the power of the Holy Spirit.

Suppose there were no examples of men and women who

have, in some unique way, manifested the traits we are talking about. Who, then, would seek after that which no one has found or seen in two thousand years of church history? The wonder of God is that, through the long ages, there have been men and women to whom we can point—men and women who have been filled with the Spirit of God. These were people whose lives and ministries radiated a beauty and a power we all would like to have. They were lifted above the crowd, and what gifts they had were magnified and intensified.

Such saints of God witness to two great truths for those of us who come after them, or who live among them today. They show us, first, that there are those who have obtained what we would like to have. Secondly, they make it clear that God will do for any and all others what He has done for them. They have no secret that eludes us. What *may* elude us is the desire to follow their pattern in order that we may experience the same blessing.

Let us turn our attention to some of the saints who have had what we ought to have and would like to have.

Spirit-filled Deacons

It would be imprudent and unfortunate to limit this discussion about Spirit-filled people of past ages to evangelists and great pulpiteers. Not everyone is called to one of these two vocations. What are the prospects for those less visible and prominent, those who may never preach a sermon or hold an evangelistic rally or crusade? Is there a need for them to be filled with the Spirit? What can they do with the power the Holy Spirit brings into their lives?

Acts 6 provides a splendid illustration of the filling of the Holy Spirit for those who waited on tables. "The Twelve gathered all the disciples together and said, 'It would not be right for us to neglect the ministry of the word of God in order to wait on tables. Brothers, choose seven men from among you who are known to be full of the Spirit and wisdom'" (Acts 6:2,3 NIV).

From this Scripture, certain facts emerge. The Twelve did not say or imply that waiting on tables is an inferior ministry. They were saying that God assigns different functions to different people. The Twelve were not averse to waiting on tables. But when it interfered with the major ministry to which the Spirit had called them, they saw the need for others to perform this important work. The Twelve knew they had been filled with the Spirit for preaching, and they knew that even waiting on tables required the fullness of the Holy Spirit if the work was to be done properly.

It is safe to say that not many churches and congregations ask seriously whether the candidates for the office of deacon have been filled with the Holy Spirit. If being filled with the Spirit was important in that day, it is no less important in our day. Indeed, it may be more important at a time in the church's history when many have departed from the true faith, and when the level of spirituality has dropped below an acceptable norm.

There are churches, in which evangelical convictions are paramount, of whom it also may be said that few are filled with the Holy Spirit. Part of this is due to the fact that the pulpit does not sound forth the teaching of Scripture on this subject. This partly derives from the failure of many who stand in the pulpits to be filled with the Spirit themselves! Moreover, the secularization of the church, in which people now stand over Scripture instead of letting Scripture stand over them, may also account for the low level of spirituality. Once the supernatural is called into question, or when it is regarded lightly, damage will be done to the teaching about the Spirit-filled life.

The Jonathan Edwards Family

Jonathan Edwards was one of the leading figures in the Great Awakening in America. He and Mrs. Edwards were filled with the Holy Spirit. The Edwards' progeny, for many generations after the deaths of these two Spirit-filled believers, enjoyed spiritual benefits flowing out of their lives. This family and their offspring included missionaries, clergymen, physicians, scholars, judges, and men who occupied high offices in the government of the United States.

Asa Mahan, in his book *The Baptism of the Holy Ghost,* recounted the story of the Edwardses. He wrote the following of Jonathan, who was then president of what was to become Princeton University: "President Edwards thus describes the baptism which rendered his subsequent life so divine:"

One day when walking for divine contemplation and prayer, I had a view, that for me was extraordinary, of the glory of the Son of God, as Mediator between God and man, and his wonderful, great, full, pure, and sweet grace and love, and meek and wonderful condescension. This grace, that appeared so calm and sweet, appeared also great above the heavens; the person of Christ appeared also ineffably excellent, with an excellency great enough to swallow up all thought and conception, and which continued, as near as I can judge, about an hour, which kept me the greater part of the time in a flood of tears, weeping aloud. I had an ardency of soul to be, what I know not otherwise how to express, emptied and annihilated, to lie in the dust and to be filled with Christ alone, to love him, and to be perfectly sanctified, and made pure with a divine and heavenly purity [p. 85].

Of Mrs. Edwards, Asa Mahan wrote, "Of the lady who afterwards became his wife, and who, during her married life, often had visions of the divine glory and love, under the power of which she would lie helpless for hours, President Edwards thus writes:"

They say there is a young lady in ————— who is beloved of that great Being who moves and rules the world, and that there are certain seasons in which this great Being, in some way or other invisible, comes to her, and fills her mind with exceeding sweet delights, and that she hardly ever cares for anything except to meditate on Him; that she expects after a while to be received up where He is, to be raised out of this world and caught up into heaven, being assured that He loves her too well to let her remain at a distance from Him always. There she is to dwell with Him, and to be ravished with His love and delight forever. Therefore, if you present all the world before her, with the richest of its treasures, she disregards it, and cares not for it, and is unmindful of any pain or affliction. She has a strange sweetness in her mind, and singular purity in her affections; is most just and conscientious in her conduct, and you could not persuade her to do anything wrong or sinful if you were to give her all the world, lest she should offend this great Being. She is of a wonderful sweetness, calmness, and benevolence of mind. She will sometimes go about from place to place, singing devoutly, and seems to be always full of joy and pleasure, and no one knows for what. She loves to be alone, walking in the fields and groves, and seems to have someone invisible always conversing with her [pp. 85–86].

Frances Ridley Havergal

Frances Ridley Havergal lived for only forty-two years. Her short life was marked by an intense commitment to Jesus Christ—a commitment that found its highest moment when she was filled with the Spirit of God. One of her biographers, Thomas Darlow, speaks of her mighty influence as a song writer, a musician, and a cheerful saint of God; as one "overshadowed and filled with the fruitful power of the Spirit of God."

There is no Protestant Christian hymnal that does not have some of her hymns and songs in it. Many lives have been blessed by her poetic gifts. Among the continuing favorites are, "I Am Trusting Thee, Lord Jesus," "Like A River Glorious," "Who Is on the Lord's Side?", "Take My Life and Let It Be," "True-Hearted, Whole-Hearted," "Lord, Speak to Me," and "Thy Life Was Given for Me."

Miss Havergal was a devout servant of Jesus Christ. In her later years, she had a profound experience in which she completely yielded to Jesus Christ and was filled to all fullness by the Spirit of God. She came under the influence of one of the great spiritual movements of that day in England. The Reverend Mr. Pennefather, vicar of St. Jude's, Mildmay Park, invited Dwight Lyman Moody to England for revival meetings. Pennefather was already leading the spiritual movement at the Mildmay Conference Hall. His ministry was devoted to what was called The Higher Christian Life. Flowing from this movement, English Keswick came into existence. And Miss Havergal was involved in all of this.

Miss Havergal wrote the following about her experience:

On Advent Sunday, December 2, 1873, I first saw clearly the blessedness of true consecration. I saw it as a flash of electric light, and what you see you can never unsee. There must be full surrender before there can be full blessedness. God admits you by one into the other. . . . so I just yielded myself to Him and utterly trusted Him to keep me. . . . That sanctification is the work of the Holy Spirit is the very thing I see and rejoice in. . . . "Sinlessness" belongs only to Christ now, and to our glorified state in heaven. . . . But being kept from falling, kept from sins, is quite another thing, and the Bible seems to teem with commands and promises about it. . . . I am so conscious of His direct teaching and guidance, through His Word and Spirit, in the matter that I cannot think that I can ever unsee it again [Thomas H. Darlow, *Frances Ridley Havergal* (Old Tappan, N.J.: Revell, 1927), pp. 34–39].

Some months later Miss Havergal wrote,

The wonderful and glorious blessing, which so many Christians are testifying to having found, was suddenly, marvellously, sent to me last winter; and life is now what I never imagined life on earth could be, though I knew much of peace and joy in believing . . . [Ibid.].

On June 3, 1879, her earthly pilgrimage was to give way to eternal felicitude in the presence of Christ she loved and adored so passionately. On the day of her death she was heard to say, "There hath not failed one word of all His good promise." Indeed she had entered into that Beulah land some years before her homegoing. The radiance of her life, the beauty of her poetry, and her sense of the presence of the Holy Spirit are part of the legacy she left behind her for Christians everywhere to read about—and to experience what she entered into if they are willing to yield to the lordship of Christ and to receive the blessing of the Spirit's presence in power and great glory.

Charles G. Finney

The life and ministry of Charles G. Finney have stood the test of the years. As an evangelist, he was without a peer. As an educator, he left his mark on America for more than a century. In the span of a single year (1857–1858) more than a hundred thousand people came to Jesus Christ, either directly or indirectly, through Finney's labors. It has been estimated that 85 percent of Finney's converts remained true to the faith they embraced. The spiritual secret that explains the powerful impact of Finney is that he was filled with the Holy Spirit. It was an episode that followed his conversion and led to his becoming an evangelist with mighty power. His own record of what happened is this:

> After dinner we [Squire Wright and himself] were engaged in removing the books and furniture to another office. We were very busy in this, and had but little conversation all the afternoon. My mind, however, remained in that profoundly tranquil state. There was a great sweetness and tenderness in my thoughts and feelings. Everything appeared to be going right, and nothing seemed to disturb me or ruffle me in the least.
>
> Just before evening the thought took possession of my mind, that as soon as I was left alone in the new office, I would try to pray again—that I was not going to abandon the subject of religion and give it up, at any rate; and therefore, although I no longer had any concern about my soul, still, I would continue to pray.
>
> By evening we got the books and furniture adjusted; and I made up, in an open fire-place, a good fire, hoping to spend the evening alone. Just at dark Squire W————, seeing that everything was adjusted, bade me good-night and went to his home. I had accompanied him to the door; and as I closed the door and turned around, my heart seemed to be liquid within me. All my feelings seemed to rise and flow out; and the utterance of my heart was, "I want to pour my whole soul out to God." The rising of my soul was so great that I rushed into the room back of the front office, to pray.
>
> There was no fire, and no light, in the room; nevertheless it appeared to me as if it were perfectly light. As I went in and shut the door after me, it seemed as if I met the Lord Jesus Christ face to face. It did not occur to me then, nor did it for some time afterward, that it was wholly a mental state. On the contrary it seemed to me that I saw Him as I would see any other man. He said nothing, but looked at me in such a manner as to break me right down at His feet. I have always since regarded this as a most remarkable state of mind; for it seemed to me a reality, that He

stood before me, and I fell down at His feet and poured out my soul to Him. I wept aloud like a child, and made such confession as I could with my choked utterance. It seemed to me that I bathed His feet with my tears; and yet I had no distinct impression that I touched Him, that I recollect.

I must have continued in this state for a good while; but my mind was too much absorbed with the interview to recollect anything that I said. But I know, as soon as my mind became calm enough to break off from the interview, I returned to the front office, and found that the fire that I had made of large wood was nearly burned out. But as I turned and was about to take a seat by the fire, *I received a mighty baptism of the Holy Ghost* [my italics]. Without any expectation of it, without ever having the thought in my mind that there was any such thing for me, without any recollection that I had ever heard the thing mentioned by any person in the world, the Holy Ghost descended on me in a manner that seemed to go through me, body and soul. I could feel the impression, like a wave of electricity, going through and through me. Indeed it seemed to come in waves and waves of liquid love; for I could not express it in any other way. It seemed like the very breath of God. I can recollect distinctly that it seemed to fan me, like immense wings.

No words can express the wonderful love that was shed abroad in my heart. I wept aloud with joy and love; and I do not know but I should say, I literally bellowed out the unutterable gushings of my heart. The waves came over me, and over me one after another, until I recollect I cried out, 'I shall die if these waves continue to pass over me.' I said, 'Lord I cannot bear any more'; yet I had no fear of death. [J. Gilchrist Lawson, *Deeper Experiences of Famous Christians*, 1911, p. 248 ff.]

This work of the Holy Spirit in the life of Finney wrought an amazing change in his life and ministry. From that moment onward he had the endowment of the Holy Spirit, who gave him the gift of an evangelist, and he had the power of the Spirit, which was the Spirit's enduement. When he talked to people they came under deep conviction of sin. Almost immediately, there was a revival in the church where Finney attended. Shortly thereafter, all of Finney's former companions, with the exception of one, came to a saving knowledge of Jesus Christ.

In the case of Finney, the Holy Spirit's work was accompanied by physical manifestations. When in the pulpit, Finney felt at times, as though he was being lifted off his feet. So excellent was the power of the Spirit working through Finney, that many people wept under the Spirit's convicting power, simply by looking at him.

It is imperative to recognize that the work of the Spirit in endowment and enduement does not necessarily extend to other areas of the Christian life and ministry. Many solid theologians have disagreed with some of the things that Finney wrote in his *Systematic Theology*. The fullness of the Spirit does not mean that the recipient becomes an infallible treasury of theological knowledge, or that all he concludes about the teachings of the Scriptures will make him perfect in his understanding. There is an endowment of the Spirit in the realm of the theological, by which special illumination is given to some to understand the deep mysteries of that discipline. Moreover, the fullness of the Spirit does not mean that all those who are filled will be given the gift of an evangelist.

The life of Finney has valuable lessons for all believers. One is that the Holy Spirit does fill Christians. The second is that the Spirit does give both gifts and power. The third is that the fullness is available for all who wish to have it. The fourth is that signs often accompany the filling of the Spirit. The fifth is that Finney was never known to have spoken in tongues, yet he had the fullness of the Spirit. Thus, tongues cannot be *the* sign of the Spirit's fullness although they may be *a* sign of the filling. Sixth, we must note that Finney wrote that he had received a mighty baptism of the Holy Spirit.

Different people have used different expressions for the experiences, as has been stated earlier. We must never suppose that the nomenclature is of supreme importance, and differences of opinion on that subject should not dispose us to repudiate something as important as this, just because some use a nomenclature that others may find questionable.

This much can be said about Charles Finney. Whatever he had, we all need. And if what he had is available to all in a variety of gifts, we ought to seek the Spirit's fullness, knowing that God graciously worked in the life of this man despite his apparent lack of biblical knowledge concerning the work of the Holy Spirit at the time of his experience.

Dwight Lyman Moody

Dwight Lyman Moody was one of the world's great evangelists. He was not a well educated man, nor did he ever attain to any perfection in the use of the English language. He never became a polished preacher. But God often uses the most unlikely people to accomplish His purposes, for then the glory more obviously belongs to Him.

Moody was first denied membership in a church because he was not sufficiently versed in the Christian faith. Several men were appointed to instruct him. Two years after his conversion experience, Moody went to Chicago and became a member of the Plymouth Congregational Church. Then, from 1856 to 1871, he worked hard as a shoe salesman and was quite successful in his labors. During the Civil War he worked as a chaplain among the soldiers, returning to Chicago when the war was over. He then made a trip to Britain, only to return to the United States with a hunger for something he wanted but did not have. He was not aware of what it was he needed.

Moody became the pastor of the largest church in Chicago, and many were the numbers of those who found Christ under his preaching. But something was lacking. He noticed two women in the congregation who sat on the front pew. They spent their time praying for Moody. When the services were over, they would tell him that they had been praying for him. Mr. Moody's rejoinder was, "Why don't you pray for the people?" They told him they prayed for him because he needed the power of the Spirit.

He was not only surprised, he was chagrined. He thought he had the power. His ministry, humanly speaking, was successful. But the remarks of the women made him think. They came to talk with him. They prayed earnestly for him, that he might be filled with the Holy Spirit. He hungered for what they were talking about. He wanted the power he felt he needed for God's service.

Then came the Chicago fire. Farwell Hall and the Illinois Street Church were burned to the ground. Moody went to New York City to seek money for the suffering people of Chicago who had lost all in the fire. He said,

> My heart was not in the work of begging. I could not appeal. I was crying all the time that God would fill me with His Spirit. Well, one day, in the city of New York—oh, what a day!—I cannot describe it. I seldom refer to it; it is almost too sacred an experience to name. Paul had an experience of which he never spoke for fourteen years. I can only say that God revealed himself to me, and I had such an experience of His love I had to ask him to stay His hand. I went to preaching again. The sermons were not different; I did not present any new truths; and yet hundreds were converted. I would not now be placed back where I was before that blessed experience if you should give me all the world—it would be as the small dust in the balance [John R. Rice, *The Power of Pentecost*, p. 393].

Dwight Moody was so overtaken by the Spirit of God that he went to the home of a friend in New York and asked for the use of a room where he could be alone with God. It was a time of blessed fellowship as the Holy Spirit swept over him again and again. He had agonized for some time before this event happened. But when it did happen, Mr. Moody had to give himself over in complete surrender to the lordship of Christ. His sense of self-sufficiency, his pride in his earlier accomplishments had to be burned at the foot of the cross. He was a transformed man from that time forward. He never mentioned speaking in tongues, nor did he ever claim that he was a perfected Christian. And as with many Christian writers of his era, Moody did not spell out various "requirements" to be filled with the Spirit as we often tend to do today. He seemed more concerned to call people to pray for and receive the power of the Spirit for service than to explain in any great detail the theology of the Spirit's work.

Reuben Archer Torrey

A. M. Hills, in his book, *Holiness and Power,* said that he "wrote a letter to Bro. Torrey, of Chicago, a month ago, asking him to tell me how he came to seek the baptism of the Holy Spirit, and what the blessing had done for him. He replied as follows:"

> I was led to seek the baptism of the Holy Spirit because I became convinced from the study of the Acts of the Apostles that no one had a right to preach the gospel until he had been baptized with the Holy Spirit. At last I was led to the place where I said that I would never enter the pulpit again until I had been baptized with the Holy Ghost and knew it, or until God in some other way told me to go. I obtained the blessing in less than a week. If I had understood the Bible as I do now there need not have passed any days.
>
> As to what the blessing has done for me, I could not begin to tell. It has brought a joy into my soul that I never dreamed of before; a liberty in preaching that makes preaching an unspeak-

able delight where before it was a matter of dread; it has opened to me a door of usefulness, so that now, instead of preaching to a very little church, I have calls every year to proclaim the truth to many thousands, being invited to conventions in every part of the land to address vast audiences; and I have a church today, in addition to my work in the Institute, that has a membership of upwards of thirteen hundred, with an evening audience that sometimes overflows the auditorium of the church, into which we can pack twenty-five hundred people, into the lecture-room below [pp. 337–38].

Charles Haddon Spurgeon

One example that illustrates what the Spirit does for a clergyman is seen in the life of Charles Haddon Spurgeon. Not only was he filled with the Spirit, but he was constrained to preach about it to the throngs who filled the tabernacle where he ministered the Word of the living God.

The content of some of what he preached may be found in his book, *Twelve Sermons of the Holy Spirit.* In the sermon titled, "The Outpouring of the Holy Spirit," he wrote,

Let the preacher always confess before he preaches that he relies on the Holy Spirit. Let him burn his manuscript and depend upon the Holy Spirit. If the Spirit does not come to help him, let him be still and let the people go home and pray that the Spirit will help him next Sunday.

In another sermon in the same book, Mr. Spurgeon wrote,

. . . I want to remind you of the blessed words of the Master, "Every one that asketh receiveth; and he that seeketh findeth; and to him that knocketh it shall be opened. If the son shall ask bread of any of you that is a father, will he give him a stone? Or if he ask a fish, will he give him a serpent? If ye then, being evil, know how to give good gifts unto your children: how much more shall your heavenly Father give the Holy Spirit to them that ask him?" You see, there is a distinct promise to the children of God, that their heavenly Father will give them the Holy Spirit if they ask for His power; and that promise is made to be exceedingly strong by the instances joined to it. But he says, *"How much more* shall your heavenly Father give the Holy Spirit to them that ask him?" He makes a stronger case than that of an ordinary father. The Lord must give us the Spirit when we ask Him, for He has herein bound Himself by no ordinary pledge. He has used a simile which would bring dishonour on His own name, and that of the very grossest kind, if He did not give the Holy Spirit to them that ask Him.

It is obvious that Mr. Spurgeon was not speaking about something he himself did not possess. He was filled with the Holy Spirit. For years, both morning and evening, he preached to a packed and overflowing church. Many, many sinners came to the knowledge of the Savior through this Spirit-filled man of God.

Conclusion

Those who serve in small places are just as much in need of the Spirit's power as those who win thousands and speak to tens of thousands. Holy Spirit power does not guarantee that the possessor, immediately or later, will necessarily be what we call "successful." God has many Spirit-filled followers hidden away in places where God's glory is manifested among the few, even as the greatness of a mighty evangelist is manifested among the many. We need all kinds of Spirit-filled servants of the Lord in all kinds of places, and there is room for more to be filled and to serve.

Is it any less necessary or less useful for a wife and a mother to be filled with the Holy Spirit? Surely the children raised in the homes of fathers and mothers who are Spirit-filled will be exposed to, and influenced by, forces that are divine. We should not forget that Elizabeth was filled with the Holy Spirit, and that John the Baptist was filled with the Holy Spirit from his mother's womb (see Luke 1:15). The Holy Spirit thus exercised an active prenatal influence on John that staggers the imagination. In today's world, where the pressures of life bear down on mothers and fathers, the need for the Spirit's filling of their lives is apparent.

Do not young people also need the fullness of the Holy Spirit? In a world out of kilter, where drugs, sex, and pornography abound, Christian young people need the power of the Holy Spirit in their lives to resist the evil powers that are at work in society. The sooner young people are Spirit-filled, the better will be their choices in determining a life's work, in the living of a faithful Christian life, and in the finding of a life partner.

The husband who drives a bus, works on an assembly line, or does custodial work needs the fullness of the Holy Spirit to be the kind of worker he should be. And he should have an influence in places and among people no one else could possibly reach with a testimony to the grace of the Lord Jesus. Why should anyone teach a Sunday school class who has not been filled with the Spirit? Or why should someone keep the church's financial books unless he or she is filled with the Holy Spirit? Perhaps it might be stated this way: Should any Christian live or die without the Spirit's fullness?

Finally, it is the fullness of the Spirit in the believer's heart that makes it possible for him or her to possess, in the fullest sense, the fruit of the Spirit—love, joy, peace, longsuffering, gentleness, goodness, faith, meekness, temperance (see Gal. 5:22–23). And when Paul gave this list he went on to say, "If we live in the Spirit, let us also walk in the Spirit" (Gal. 5:25). Living and walking go hand in hand. The way to do both is to be filled with the Holy Spirit of God.

NINE
On Being Holy People

Whenever anyone discusses holiness, a host of questions and many differences of opinion surface. One school of thought is committed to what is called "eradication." They mean by this that sin has been banished and the believer of whom this is true is living a life of sinless perfection. Many of those who hold this view teach that sanctification is something that must be sought, and its attainment is often spoken of as a second work of grace.

The eradication doctrine is largely associated with groups such as the early Methodists (although among many members of the United Methodist Church today, there is virtually no emphasis on this subject), the holiness groups such as the Church of the Nazarene, the Pilgrim Holiness denomination, and others. Altar calls for holiness are given, and inquirers respond to the call with the expectation that they will be lifted to a higher spiritual plane wherein genuine holiness becomes the badge of their Christian life and walk.

Years ago in his book, *Holiness and Power for the Church and the Ministry,* Aaron Merritt Hills argued for a state of perfection, which he described as follows:

> Wonderful salvation! which so sanctifies the soul that it is "crucified to the world," and "freed" from the tendency to sin, and "dead" to all the solicitations of evil! [p. 106].

The point of tension, here, lies in the difference between the Arminian and the rigid Calvinist viewpoint concerning the nature of the daily Christian walk. Reduced to some sort of formula, one might phrase it this way: The Arminian, from the Hills perspective, is saying that when the believer is filled with the Holy Spirit he *cannot* sin; the Calvinist, on the other hand, seems to be saying that whether the believer is or is not filled with the Holy Spirit, he *will* sin in word, thought, and deed every day. There is a third option, however, which differs from both of these in a material sense, and it may provide a better answer to this difference of opinion. It can be stated this way: The believer may sin but *he does not have to.*

Using Mr. Hills's statement that the believer, when filled with the Spirit, is "'freed' from the tendency to sin and 'dead' to all solicitations of evil," the conclusion that normally would follow from such an assertion is this: that person has reached perfection and cannot sin. If he cannot sin, not only can he not lose the infilling power of the Spirit, he cannot lose his salvation; that is, he cannot fall from grace. This obviously means that he has eternal security. But eternal security is a Reformed doctrine, to which Arminians take exception. Eradication, then, is a doctrine that nullifies the Arminian objections to eternal security. Once eradication is accepted, the most the Arminian can say is that any believer can lose his salvation until such time that the second blessing has become his. After that he can no longer sin, and thus is sure of his eternal security.

If we follow the Reformed tradition that eradication or perfectionism is incorrect, what then do we mean when we speak about holiness in relation to the infilling of the Holy Spirit? Surely it must be plain that reigning or unconfessed sin is an obvious impediment to being filled with the Spirit. Earlier it was stated that the confession of all known sin must take place before anyone can pray with confidence, asking God to fill him or her with His Holy Spirit. Moreover, we have already shown that the promise of God to infill the believer is contingent upon the confession of all known sin. Whoever claims God's promise for the infilling of the Spirit without first confessing his or her sins can be sure that such a prayer will not be answered by God. But what is meant when we speak about confessing all known sin? Is it not true that when we confess our sins God is faithful and just to forgive us our sins? If we do this, are we not, at least at that moment, in a state of perfection? The answer is negative. Why do we say this?

The better term for the spiritual state of the believer who has confessed all known sin is blamelessness. By blamelessness we mean that the believer is, at that moment, free from any barrier or hindrance that would keep him or her from being filled by the Holy Spirit. But that believer is still in the flesh and *may* be tempted to sin, even though the level of resistance will have been heightened and a positive response to the solicitation will be far less likely than it was before he or she was filled with the Spirit.

In his book, Mr. Hills makes a statement that is difficult to reconcile with his argument that filled believers are dead to solicitation to sin and are freed from the tendency to sin. Speaking about what happened in the lives of two of God's saints he said, "Dear Dr. Keen and his wife sought together the enduement of 'power from on high' for seven days, and that great outpouring came that never left him until he was glorified after a quarter of a century of triumphant service" (p. 211). There would have been no need for Mr. Hills to emphasize that the infilling never left Dr. Keen if in fact it was not possible for him to lose that infilling.

Mr. Hills refers to the experience of R. A. Torrey, who was the head of Mr. Moody's school in Chicago. He used him as a great example of what he was advocating. But he made no mention whatever of Mr. Torrey's own writings on the subject of being filled with the Spirit. Torrey everywhere warned his readers that they could lose the infilling power of the Holy Spirit, and he specified what the most common sins were, which resulted in the loss of the Spirit's power.

Surely if the infilling produces a state of perfection that cannot be lost, then Mr. Torrey was mistaken when he taught that the power and blessing of the Spirit can be quenched. Nowhere did Mr. Torrey endorse sinless perfection, nor did he teach eradication.

Furthermore, the Old Testament cases we examined earlier indicate that some of those saints of God who were filled with the Holy Spirit did not attain perfection. Indeed some of them were definitely backsliders. Samson was filled with the Spirit. But he lost what he had. He was guilty of marrying an unbeliever. He consorted with a prostitute. He lived with, but apparently never married, Delilah. He broke his Nazarite vow, was blinded, and lost his power. It was only after repentance that he was restored and his strength was returned to him.

Saul, the first king of Israel, was Spirit-filled. But he sinned against God and the Spirit of God departed from him. The Spirit was effectively quenched, if you please, and Saul became a spiritual shipwreck.

Another point remains to be made. It is possible for a believer to confess all of his or her known sins without confessing sins of which he or she has no conscious awareness. The Scriptures speak of this possibility plainly. The apostle Paul said that he had no conscious awareness of anything against him, yet he was not thereby justified (1 Cor. 4:4). God alone knows the heart, and God alone justifies.

Evidence in the Old Testament Scriptures strikingly supports the same claim. Moses wrote that priests, rulers, and the common people may sin unwittingly. That is, they may break some commandment of God without doing so knowingly. But if and when it is drawn to their attention, they are commanded to offer the usual sin offering for the transgression (see Lev. 4:1ff). The grace of God covers the sins of which we have no awareness on the basis of our heart intention and desire. For if we know of the unwitting sin, we will confess it. But its existence, unknown to us, does not make it less than a sin. Thus, we must distinguish between the intention and the performance.

We surely can agree that God looks at the intention of the heart and accepts the intention for the performance when the performance is less than perfect, especially when the imperfection of the performance is unknown to us. But of whom can it be said that he has loved God with his whole heart, that is, 100 percent, without even the slightest deviation from the perfect norm? The most minute deviation from the standard of perfection constitutes sin. But where the intention to love God with the whole heart exists, God is gracious, forgiving, and loving. And He does not keep us from being filled with His Holy Spirit.

The Characteristics of a Holy Walk

The apostle Paul, in the Epistle to the Galatians, treated the subject of a believer's holy walk under the guidance and by the assistance of the Holy Spirit. He carefully enjoined the Galatians to "walk in the Spirit, and you shall not fulfill the lust of the flesh" (Gal. 5:16). His meaning becomes clearer when we call to mind what he also had to say in his first letter to the Corinthians. Paul wanted the Corinthians and the Galatians to live holy lives.

Paul wrote to the Corinthians, "And I, brethren, could not speak to you as to spiritual people but as to carnal, as to babes in Christ" (1 Cor. 3:1). The thrust of this passage is significant in that Paul recognized that some regenerated persons still lived a carnal or fleshly life. He spoke of some of their actions that revealed their carnality. But he did not say they had lost their salvation, nor did he threaten them with such a loss. Rather, he encouraged them to erect a suitable building upon the foundation of their faith in Christ. He was saying that there are carnal Christians and there are spiritual Christians. Carnal or fleshly Christians are not filled with the Spirit and do not "walk in the Spirit," as he commanded believers to do in the Galatian letter.

In Galatians Paul sharply repudiated salvation by works, that is, by keeping the law. But he nowhere said that the redeemed ought not obey the laws of God. He boldly asserted that they are free and he specified that "if you are led by the Spirit, you are not under the law" (Gal. 5:18), but because they are under Christ they are enjoined to walk in the Spirit because this is pleasing to their Lord. He clearly affirmed that the way Christians walk will tell the world whether they are living holy lives.

Paul purposed to supply Christians with a set of characteristics by which they could judge whether they were walking after the Spirit or after the flesh. He proclaimed that the works of the flesh are "adultery, fornication, uncleanness, licentiousness, idolatry, sorcery, hatred, contentions, jealousies, outbursts of wrath, selfish ambitions, dissensions, heresies, envy, murders, drunkenness, revelries, and the like" (5:19–21). The list is not exhaustive, for in the Greek it says, in addition to the specific sins named by Paul, "and (things) like to these."

This passage is not to be construed in such a way that the absence of these particular sins means believers have passed the test and are living holy lives. Believers who do not drink, carouse, or commit immorality have simply put off the works of darkness. They still have to put on the works of righteousness. Although they will not be saved by doing works of righteousness, those works will show a questioning world that they mean business with Jesus and that they have been filled with the Holy Spirit. They then will live the kind of lives made possible for all Spirit-filled believers.

Paul went on to speak of the "fruit of the Spirit." This is simply the life of holiness wrought out in believers' lives by the power of the Spirit who has filled them. The marks of a holy life are "love, joy, peace, longsuffering, kindness, goodness, faithfulness, gentleness, self-control" (Gal. 5:22–23). Fittingly, Paul remarked that those who have the marks of the Spirit are the ones who "have crucified the flesh with its passions and desires" (Gal. 5:24). Who can deny that the good characteristics mentioned by Paul are all of the kind virtually no believers have in and of themselves? They are divinely imparted or Spirit-acquired characteristics.

The bottom line for Paul was whether what we profess is identical with what we possess. He enjoined, "If we live in the Spirit, let us also walk in the Spirit" (Gal. 5:25). Living and walking go hand in hand. To assert that we have life in Christ, and then to deny the implications that flow out of that relationship by living carnal or fleshly lives, is inconsistent, even irrational. We know Paul was saying plainly that a holy people are a separated people even though they are not a perfect people. They may sin; they may even backslide. But if they do so, it is by conscious choice. They can help themselves through the power of the Spirit, but the Spirit will not force them to conform to the divine will.

At this point in his discussion, if he believed in the doctrine of perfection, Paul surely should have said that once the people of God live and walk in the Spirit, they have reached a state of perfection and cannot sin. Instead, he opened the door wide to the possibility that they may sin. He wrote, "Brethren, if a man is overtaken in any trespass, you who are spiritual, restore such a one in a spirit of gentleness, considering yourself lest you also be tempted" (Gal. 6:1). Surely Paul was warning that those believers who are to restore a fallen brother or sister should not themselves be swollen with pride. They, too, may fall into the same or similar sins. They can be tempted just as the fallen believer was tempted. This teaching does not support eradication. It presupposes that eradication awaits us when we are glorified. We are to live blameless lives, not perfect ones, using confession, repentance, and restitution to restore the fullness of the Spirit we once had.

Holiness and the Spirit-Filled Life

Should we not ask ourselves frankly whether it is possible for believers to live lives of holiness and at the same time not be filled with the Holy Spirit? The life of holiness and the infilling of the Holy Spirit go hand in hand. They cannot, and ought not, be separated.

May we sometimes possess that of which we have no particular awareness? May we either be filled with the Spirit and think less of holiness than we should, or enjoy lives of holiness without too much attention being paid to the fullness of the Spirit? I ask this because so many of the writers on the subject of holiness tie it up in one way or another to a life of power. They are saying that holiness is accompanied by a changed life with regard to service for God and the power we all need to serve Him.

It should be apparent that there can be no Spirit-filled life without holiness. This has already been stated. But holiness, or a life of blamelessness, precedes the infilling of the Spirit. It is a requirement that must be met *before* the infilling takes place. Retaining the fullness of the Spirit's power implies the necessity for maintaining this life of holiness or blamelessness.

I like to think of it by the use of the term *steady state*. By this I mean that holiness and power do not come and then go, except as we lose the infilling power of the Holy Spirit through sin. It *is* possible for any believer to remain filled with the Holy Spirit without interruption. Does this then suggest eradication, a state where the believer cannot sin and thus lose the Spirit's power? By no means. Believers can sin, and most of us do at one time or another. How can we enjoy a steady state? Two things must be said about this.

Let us remember that we claim the Spirit's power by faith. We drink at the fountain, or enjoy the rivers of living water, day by day. If we break the connection with the living waters, we are back where we were before we claimed the promise of the Spirit's fullness. I do not think it correct to say that those who have not been filled with the Spirit are guilty of living in sin. I prefer to think of such believers as simply living without claiming a promise that is theirs *if* they desire to have it. Such a person may still be blameless before the Lord, while not claiming the Spirit's power. In other words, believers can lead a holy life without the Spirit's infilling, but they cannot enjoy the Spirit's filling unless they are living a holy life. Thus, we come to the second observation.

If and when believers deliberately sin against God and do not turn immediately from that sin in repentance, confession, and restoration, they will lose the infilling of the Holy Spirit and will also lose the life of holiness or blamelessness. Indeed, the loss of holiness is always accompanied by the loss of the infilling power of the Spirit. What are some of the common sins that occasion the loss of the infilling?

Any Christian who does whatever is forbidden by the commandments of God is guilty of sin, and this results in a state of sinfulness, rather than a state of holiness. When we lie, cheat, steal, take the name of God in vain, commit fornication or adultery, we become backslidden. Pride, greed for money, or self-indulgence are also sins that defeat us in the spiritual life. Whenever we lessen our commitment to the lordship of Christ, the result will be the same. We will be powerless. All of those transgressions are of an active nature. They constitute

147

things we do. But there are other sins, which may be equally heinous, and which do not spring from outright actions. Rather, they come from things we fail to do.

Those in the Reformed tradition customarily pray, and rightly I believe, for the forgiveness of the things they have done that they should not have done. And then they pray for forgiveness for the things they should have done but failed to do. Stealing is active. Failing to read the Word of God is non-active. It is something we should do, but we do not always do it. One of the sure ways to lose the Spirit's power is the failure to hear and obey the Word of God.

God speaks to His people through the written Word of God. Except in extraordinary and unusual circumstances, God does not speak to us in an audible voice. He has already spoken in the Word of God written, and if we refuse to immerse ourselves in the Word He has given, why should we suppose that He will speak to us in some other way? Faithfulness in reading the Bible is of the utmost importance for maintaining the Spirit-filled life.

Prayer is another of the activities that, when neglected, causes us to lose the spiritual power. When we are busy at prayer and in doing what we should do, we will keep from doing what we should not do. If we love God with our whole hearts, we will be kept from a multitude of other sins. If we love our neighbors as we love ourselves, we will be at peace with them and life will move along smoothly. Doing what is right keeps us from doing what is wrong.

We may say ultimately that disobedience, in the broadest sense of that term, is the sin that causes us to lose the infilling of the Holy Spirit. All of the sins we commit or all of the duties we fail to engage in constitute disobedience. Obedience covers the negatives and the positives, the things we are to do and the things we are not to do.

Regaining the Lost Blessing

Let us suppose, for the moment, that a Spirit-filled servant of God has committed some sin and has lost the Spirit's power. Is it possible for that believer to be restored to the place and position he or she once occupied?

In his delightful little book, *The Spirit-Filled Life,* John MacNeil speaks about regaining the lost blessing. He uses the illustration of the young theological student in Elisha's time who lost the borrowed axe-head that fell into the water and appeared to be irrecoverable. Elisha asked him where he lost the axe-head. When he was told, he cut a stick and cast it in at that place. Then the iron axe-head surfaced. It was recovered. He regained it at the very spot where he lost it.

The moral of the story is plain enough. Once the student had lost the axe-head he could not go on chopping until he got the axe-head again. When we sin and lose the infilling power of the Spirit, we must go back to the place where we lost the power. There we can find it again.

There are times and circumstances when the sin a believer commits is of such a nature that it becomes disenabling. Let us examine, for example, what happens when a minister of the gospel is known to have committed adultery. Is this a forgivable sin? Of course it is. But should such a man be permitted to continue in the gospel ministry? Or does this sort of sin disenable him from filling the office of pastor of the sheep?

Such a person, under the Old Testament law, would have been stoned to death. Today, we do not stone people to death for adultery. Such a person, however, should not be permitted to continue in his office as a minister of the gospel. He should be defrocked. Never again should he be entrusted with this responsibility. Repentance, confession, and refilling with the Spirit may well occur. But the errant party can never recover from his loss of the role model of righteousness he previously enjoyed. His usefulness as a minister of the gospel is forever impaired.

Let us observe another case. Suppose a believer is the head of a Christian organization. His marriage falls apart and divorce results. It is not caused by adultery or by desertion. The partners simply agree to separate. Should this person, who stands as a model for ministry, continue in his office?

In our day, the standards of conduct have been lowered far beyond what Scripture permits. From the biblical perspective, it appears that such a person should no longer labor as the head of an organization that regards divorce as forbidden by the Word of God. But suppose the man is an innocent victim who has done no wrong. His wife is the one who breaks the marriage. She refuses to live with him. The consequence is the same. No one can ever be sure what was the true cause of the separation. Nor can blame be established that easily. Such a person, regardless of the circumstances, should be removed from the responsibility of office.

Is it fair to "penalize" the innocent party? Whether we like it or not, each life is bound up with other lives, and the sins of any one of us may produce disastrous consequences in the lives of others. Any Christian leader who has influence in the lives of others should step down from that position when his example is marred by public sin.

The apostle Paul stated that a man who aspires to the office of bishop must keep "his children in submission with all reverence" (1 Tim. 3:4). In other words if his children are not like this, he ought not seek, or be appointed to, or remain in the office of bishop. Thus, wicked children can bring disenablement to their father.

Whoever is Spirit-filled must be keenly aware that if and when he sins, there are consequences that flow from it. No one can take it for granted that the departure of the Spirit's power, or the quenching of the Spirit, can be overlooked by God. There were consequences of the sin in the lives of Ananias and Sapphira. There was a deadly pay day in the life of Samson. He did find deliverance, and he recovered from his transgression; he was refilled with the power of the Spirit. He was enabled to perform another mighty physical act, but he lost his life and ended his possibility for further ministry.

No one who is filled with the Spirit wants to be a spiritual shipwreck. But the possibility of this needs to be kept before us as a preventive, so that, when tempted, we will automatically look for and experience the power of the Spirit to deliver us from temptation. In this way, we may continue the *steady state* of an unbroken fellowship with the Father, the Son, and the Holy Spirit.

The saints of God in the holiness movement in past years have made a great contribution to our understanding of the life of power. Those of us who cannot find eradication in their understanding of Scripture should not therefore lose the blessing of much that is contained in the holiness doctrine. For without holiness, no one shall see the Lord (see Heb. 12:14). And unless there is genuine holiness of life, as we have underscored it here in the notion of blamelessness, there can be no Spirit-filled life worthy of the name. We should not lost sight of the notion contained in the idea of eradication, which supports the possibility of a *steady state* experience. By this experience believers may walk hand in hand with the Father, Son, and the Holy Spirit and do so, moment by moment, across the long days of this life's journey.

Tongues (glossolalia), Holiness, and the Baptism in the Holy Spirit

We need to consider the role of speaking in tongues in the Spirit-filled life (called "the Baptism in the Holy Ghost [Spirit]" by the Assemblies of God). This cannot be separated from holiness, of which we have been talking, but what the relationship is needs to be established. The Assemblies of God denomination is fairly representative of the pentecostal groups in the United States. In their antecedents there are connections with the holiness movement, but that relationship has faded in the last half century.

So far as I know, few, if any, of the holiness groups have tied their holiness doctrine to speaking in tongues as the only evidence that holiness has come upon the believer. Indeed, few of the holiness people say much about the baptism in the Holy Ghost *per se*. As we have already seen, the infilling by the Spirit or the baptism in the Spirit (for behind the nomenclature there is something all agree exists) is related to a life of holiness or blamelessness. But what does speaking in tongues have to do with all of this?

Section 7, in the statement of beliefs of the Assemblies of God is entitled "The Baptism in the Holy Ghost." It reads as follows:

> All believers are entitled to and should ardently expect and earnestly seek the promise of the Father, the baptism in the Holy Ghost and fire, according to the command of our Lord Jesus Christ. This was the normal experience of all in the early Christian Church. With it comes the enduement of power for life and service, the bestowment of the gifts and their uses in the work of the ministry (Luke 24:49; Acts 1:4,8: I Corinthians 12:1–31). This experience is distinct from and subsequent to the experience of the new birth (Acts 8:12–17; 10:44–46; 11:14–15; 15:7–9). With the baptism in the Holy Ghost come such experiences as an overflowing fullness of the Spirit (John 7:37–39; Acts 4:8), a deepened reverence for God (Acts 2:43; Hebrews 12:28), an intensified consecration to God and dedication to His work (Acts 2:42), and a more active love for Christ, for His Word, and for the lost (Mark 16:20).

Section 8 of the statement is entitled "The Evidence of the Baptism in the Holy Ghost" and reads as follows:

> The baptism of believers in the Holy Ghost is witnessed by the initial physical sign of speaking with other tongues as the Spirit gives them utterance (Acts 2:4). The speaking in tongues in this instance is the same in essence as the gift of tongues (I Corinthians 12:4–10,28), but different in purpose and use.

Then Section 9 is entitled "Sanctification" and reads as follows:

> Sanctification is an act of separation from that which is evil and of dedication unto God (Romans 12:1,2; I Thessalonians 5:23; Hebrews 13:12). The Scriptures teach a life of "holiness without which no man shall see the Lord" (Hebrews 12:14). By the power of the Holy Ghost we are able to obey the command: "Be ye holy, for I am holy" (I Peter 1:15,16).
>
> Sanctification is realized in the believer by recognizing his identification with Christ in His death and resurrection, and by faith reckoning daily upon the fact of that union, and by offering every faculty continually to the dominion of the Holy Spirit (Romans 6:1–11,13; 18(sic):1,2,13; Galatians 2:20; Phil. 2:12,13; I Peter 1:5).

First and foremost we must state what the essential components of these statements are.

1. The baptism in the Holy Spirit occurs subsequent to the experience of the new birth.
2. Nothing in the entire statement speaks about the first baptism, in which the new believer is baptized into the body of Christ. Nor is there any statement about the sealing of the believer and the indwelling of the believer by the Holy Spirit. The statement does not say when sealing and indwelling occur, that is, at the time of the baptism in the Holy Spirit, or at the time of conversion and the new birth.
3. The witness to the baptism in the Holy Spirit is speaking

in tongues. From this statement it is clear that whoever has not spoken in tongues has not been baptized in the Holy Spirit. Tongues is *the* sign of the baptism, not *a* sign of the baptism.

4. The results that flow from being baptized in the Spirit are stated—"overflowing fullness of the Spirit," "a deepened reverence for God," "an intensified consecration to God and dedication to His work," "and a more active love for Christ, for His Word, and for the lost." The conclusion can be fairly drawn that those who have not spoken in tongues will not and cannot manifest these characteristics. If they can, then the baptism in the Spirit and speaking in tongues become superfluous, that is, they are not needed to enjoy those things described. On the other hand, if it was the intention to say that these things exist in a believer's heart before the baptism, but are deepened or intensified after the baptism, it is confusing and implicitly contradictory.

5. The two statements dealing with the baptism in the Spirit do not state explicitly what the relationship of this is to sanctification or to a life of holiness. However, the statement on sanctification does say that believers can only live holy lives through the power of the Holy Spirit. Since power is part of the baptism in the Spirit, this would seem to tie holiness to the baptism and suggest that where there is no baptism in the Spirit, true holiness will not exist. If it is possible to live a genuine life of holiness without enjoying the baptism in the Spirit, then the holiness would be defective for the following reason. If the baptism in the Spirit is commanded by God, then whoever does not have it is disobedient and is falling short of an express command of God. This would be no less offensive to God than stealing or lying, and perhaps more so, since it involves something regarded as of the highest significance.

Some statistics are available that throw light on the relationship between speaking in tongues and holiness. In the February 22, 1980, issue of *Christianity Today*, some statistics derived from a Gallup Poll sponsored by the magazine were reported.

Eighty-six percent of those polled who said they spoke in tongues were Protestants. Nineteen percent of those who spoke in tongues said they approved of sexual relations before marriage. This can only mean that one out of every five who spoke in tongues in 1979 had a defective view of the biblical teaching about sex before marriage. Such believers have a rather odd view about the life of holiness. Thus, for many, tongues is of no particular help in their understanding of holiness.

Forty-six percent of those who spoke in tongues did not hold that the Bible is the most important religious authority. Fourteen percent acknowledged they did not "hold the Bible as the Word of God and not mistaken in its statements and teaching." Thirty-seven percent were not tithers. Thirteen percent did not read the Bible weekly. Twenty-four percent did not attend church services weekly. Fifty-one percent did not talk about faith at least weekly. Fifty-eight percent did not "set priority on winning the world for Christ." Twenty-nine percent used alcoholic beverages. Fifteen percent did not "hold that the only hope for heaven is through personal faith in Jesus Christ." All of the people mentioned above claimed to have spoken in tongues. Five million claimed this gift.

What conclusions can we draw from these statistics? Obviously, some tongues speaking is either counterfeit, demonic, or is not being accompanied by a life in submission to God's will. We can conclude, then, that there is a claim to the gift of tongues by people who are not living lives of holiness. Spiritual gifts can be displayed by unholy people (see Matt. 7:22–23).

This is dismaying, but true. A substantial number of people who speak in tongues apparently are negligent (as are believers who don't have the gift) in regard to tithing, reading the Word of God, attending church services regularly, and having a missionary vision.

This same article reads: ". . . studies show that from 50 to 66 percent of classical Pentecostal church members who accept Pentecostal teachings and who are full members of a Pentecostal denomination that is committed to Pentecostal distinctives have never spoken in tongues." The implications of this statement alone are staggering. Apparently vast numbers of the members of pentecostal churches are wanting in one of the chief emphases of their denominations. Moreover, it is apparent that the churches themselves are unsuccessful in getting their parish members to receive the baptism with the Holy Spirit. This is especially unusual among people who base their claim for speaking in tongues on what is recorded in the Acts of the Apostles.

Why do I say this? In the Upper Room incident, all of the participants were baptized or filled with the Holy Spirit. In Acts 8, everyone who was there in the Samaria incident received the Holy Spirit (see Acts 8:17). In Acts 10:44, "the Holy Spirit fell on *all those* who heard the word" (italics mine). And in the mention of the filling by the Holy Spirit in Acts 11:14–15 and 15:7–9, there is not a word which suggests that only some experienced the blessing. This overall experience is not happening among the pentecostal churches today. A few here and there receive the blessing, but multitudes have never enjoyed this experience. If the Acts of the Apostles record is normative, then the Holy Spirit should fall on all who are present every time the infilling occurs in a local congregation.

At the heart of the tongues issue lies the claim that speaking in tongues is the only sign of the baptism in the Holy Ghost. Can this be demonstrated from Scripture? A goodly number of

God's servants across the years have not found this to be taught in Scripture as normative. Some, incorrectly, think there can be no tongues in this age in any event. The chief passage on tongues (see 1 Cor. 12) appears to be very plain. Paul described the varieties of gifts, all of which are given by the Spirit, "distributing to each one individually as He wills" (v. 11).

The recurring phrase, "to one is given . . . to another is given," makes it clear that no one gift is given, or even made available, to all believers. Paul specifically said that "to another different kinds of tongues" are given. Later on, he was even more specific when he asked, "Are all apostles? . . . Do all speak with tongues?" (vv. 29–30). These rhetorical questions were asked within a context that indicates with certitude that not all speak or will speak in tongues, and not all who do not speak in tongues are to be considered less spiritual or lacking in something needful.

Moreover, we should not suppose we are all made in the same mold. God, who has made every leaf of every tree different from every other leaf, made each one of us different from every other human being. It is hardly likely that the vast number of evangelicals who do not endorse tongues as *the* sign of the Spirit's infilling will change their views. However, believers who hold this view should not refuse to accept the reality that lies behind tongues, a reality that is most important for every Christian to receive from God. I refer here to the endowment and the enduement of the Holy Spirit. The baptism with the Spirit is not designed primarily to make us happy, nor is it given to make us proud. It is designed to empower us for service to God.

Holiness and tongues cannot be dismissed lightly. But it is equally important to make plain that the *general* evangelical understanding of holiness does not include the idea of eradication or perfection. And the acceptance of the undeniable fact that some people do receive the gift of tongues does not go as far as that of many pentecostals who teach that it is the only valid sign of the baptism with the Spirit. Nor do evangelicals generally think that all Christians can or will be given the gift of speaking in tongues by the Holy Spirit.

Beneath these differences of opinion should be lives marked by love for those who are, in every sense, true believers and whom God has blessed in an abundant fashion. The differences should not be thought of as constituting an assault on the fundamentals of the Christian faith, nor should they be considered a hindrance to genuine fellowship under the lordship of Jesus Christ. The happy truth is that people of these persuasions and those who differ with them have met, and do meet, under the umbrella of the National Association of Evangelicals and other agencies and will continue to do so in the years ahead. The longstanding principle should be upheld and practiced: In the fundamentals of the faith there must be unity; in other matters there must be love in the midst of diversity.

TEN

Eight Questions Often Asked about the Filling of the Holy Spirit

When we speak about being filled with the Holy Spirit, certain questions must be considered. They are questions any thinking person is more than likely to ask, not by way of doubts, but for learning and spiritual movement.

1. *Is there only one filling of the Holy Spirit, or are there many fillings? Are there "refillings?"*
Surely these questions must be asked.

The various uses of the Greek root word for *filling* throw some light on these questions. The Greek language has the aorist tense for verbs, which we do not have in the English language. This Greek tense reflects something that happens, and as soon as it does happen, it is a complete act. It represents a sudden, definite action of the past.

This can be illustrated in Acts 2:4, where the Scripture says that all of the believers assembled in the upper room were "filled with the Holy Spirit." Something happened. And when it happened, it was a finished or completed action. Peter was among those who were filled at that time. The word used for this filling experience is *eplesthesan*. The same Greek word is used again in Acts 4:31. All who were there were filled. Peter and others of those who had been filled in the upper room were filled again here. What does this tell us?

We can conclude one of several things. One possibility is that being filled with the Spirit is something that occurs again and again. If this is so, then being filled with the Spirit is indeterminate. It may last for a moment, for an hour, or for a day. In that event, the believer is faced constantly with the need to seek for a new infilling. It would thus be impossible to enjoy a steady state of being filled and being kept filled as a normal condition of living in the Spirit.

This possibility is hardly acceptable. Yet, we must find a resolution to the problem that Peter is said to have been filled a second time, not too long after Pentecost.

Perhaps the experience of the apostle Paul provides us with the best answer to this dilemma. In Acts 9:17, Paul was filled with the Spirit for the first time. This filling occurred shortly after his actual conversion on the road to Damascus, when he met Jesus in a special confrontation. In Acts 13:9, he was filled again with the Spirit, and the same Greek word is used to describe what happened.

The key here is that Paul was face to face with the necessity of speaking hard words to Elymas the Sorcerer. This presented Paul with a severe test and a substantial challenge. He needed special power for this moment. And he needed it to challenge the forces of darkness whom Elymas served. This might, then, be called a new infilling, or a refilling, or a response by the Spirit to a time of special need in the life and ministry of the apostle. He was already filled with the Spirit, but in this crisis situation, he needed to have special power above that which he possessed from day to day.

The Scripture, in this instance, states that Paul was "filled with the Holy Spirit," and the Greek tense is the aorist, which is finished action. And when this happened, Paul opened his mouth and said, "You son of the devil, you enemy of all righteousness, will you not cease perverting the straight ways of the Lord? And now, indeed, the hand of the Lord is upon you, and you shall be blind, not seeing the sun for a time" (Acts 13:10–11).

That particular situation, in which Paul engaged in a great battle with a man filled with the power of Satan, required a special anointing, or what we can rightly call the refilling of the Holy Spirit, which was given to him for this emergency situation. As in the case of Isaiah 49:2, "He has made My mouth like a sharp sword," so the mouth of Paul was like a sharp sword as he strove against the host of spiritual wickedness in high places. The lesson to be learned, of course, is that all the power of the Spirit that we need for any and all occasions is available to us at any time by a special work of the Holy Spirit.

There is still another possibility in the confrontation between Paul and Elymas that is worthy of exploration. The Holy Spirit may give us a permanent gift among those listed earlier. Thus, for example, a minister of the gospel needs the gift of prophecy, which has for its controlling principle, the ability to understand and preach the Word of God. The same Spirit may then give to the same believer one-time gifts required for special situations. Such a believer might be given the gift of faith or the gift of healing on a special occasion. Thus, the gift of healing might be given in a single instance.

We cannot box in the Holy Spirit. When we read that the disciples were filled with the Spirit in Acts 4, what was the difference between that second one, and their first experience at Pentecost? In the first experience they were given the gift of tongues. In the second one, we are not told that they spoke in tongues. However, they were given other gifts that were different from those given at Pentecost. They were given a unity, and grace was upon them, and they became liberal givers far beyond the normal tithe (see Acts 4:32–35). (In this instance of extraordinary giving, there is no principle or precedent for socialism, nor is it a normative model for all believers for all time. The same Spirit, however, could do something similar today in the heart of a single believer, or He could move a group of believers or a local church to heights of sacrificial beneficence.)

And what about "refillings"? Do we have to keep on being filled with the Spirit, or is there a state or condition by which we can say that we are filled and remain filled with the Spirit for an indeterminate period of time? What about experiences like those of Paul and Peter who, when faced with difficult circumstances, needed a fresh or special anointing of the Spirit?

It seems to me that the Scripture teaches what I call elsewhere in this book, the *steady state*. In Acts 6:3, we read that seven men were to be chosen to fill the new office created for the churches, the office of deacon. The requirements for filling the office are stated plainly: "Seek out from among you seven men . . . full of the Holy Spirit" (Acts 6:3). The word *full* is found in other places. In Acts 6:5, and 7:55, Stephen is said to be full of the Holy Spirit. In Acts 11:24, Barnabas is said to be "full of the Holy Spirit."

In these cases, it appears that being full of the Holy Spirit was the normal condition of their lives. Instead of static and isolated "refillings," we have here dynamic, connected, continual freshness of the Spirit day by day, task by task. If believers can be full of the Holy Spirit, and if this signifies the steady state of which we have spoken, then it follows that holiness must be a characteristic of the steady state.

2. What are some of the results or effects of being filled with the Holy Spirit?

The fruit of the Spirit is one of the consequences flowing out of the fullness of the Spirit (see Gal. 5:22–23). Is it not difficult to suppose that anyone can really produce the fruit of the Spirit, in the best and fullest sense of that term, unless one is filled with the Holy Spirit in the first place?

Love is mentioned first in the description of the fruit of the

Spirit. Love characterized the believers immediately after the pentecostal experience. We return to Acts 4 again. Whoever in the early church had needs had them supplied by others who had more than they needed. Because of their love, "nor was there anyone among them who lacked" (Acts 4:34), for "they distributed to each as anyone had need" (Acts 4:35). This was love at work.

It was not something done for those outside the household of faith. It did not mean that the disciples set up a society in which there was equal sharing so that egalitarianism was the order of the day. It was simply that those who had genuine economic needs were helped by others who had more, who shared what they had out of their love for each other.

Nor did it allow for slackers and indigents to expect others to do for them what they were supposed to do for themselves. Elsewhere Paul stated that whoever would not work should not eat. Love is stern as well as giving. No one is made stronger by being subsidized when he or she is able to work. Certainly Christians should display their love for each other as Paul later did, when he took up an offering for the poor saints at Jerusalem from the richer saints at Corinth. In 1 Corinthians 16:1–5, Paul wrote about taking their gift to Jerusalem for the saints there.

The fruit of the Spirit also includes the joy of the Lord. The disciples were filled with gladness: they ate what they had with thanksgiving and singleness of heart. They rejoiced that they were counted worthy to suffer for Christ's sake. When persecuted, they were filled with joy. When Paul and Silas were in prison, they sang songs in the night. They experienced the peace of God. It is the fruit of the Spirit, then, that characterizes the lives of those who are Spirit-filled.

3. *How does being filled with the Holy Spirit change our actions, the things we* do, *as we live our daily lives?*

Perhaps we need to realize afresh that Paul's injunction to the Ephesians (5:18) to be filled with the Spirit is followed closely by a series of tests that would tell them whether they have been filled with the Spirit. They would know it by the change of life that sprang from the filling.

In 5:19, the Ephesians are to have singing hearts; in verse 20, they are to be thankful to God. In verse 21, they are to have submissive hearts, in which they do not hesitate to be subject one to another. In verse 22, Spirit-filled women gladly submit to their husbands, who are to head up the house. According to verse 25, Spirit-filled husbands are to love their wives as Jesus Christ loves His church.

In Ephesians 6:1, Spirit-filled children (and children can and should be filled with the Spirit) should obey their parents. Interestingly, in Paul's second letter to Timothy, he specifically stated that in the end times, children will be "disobedient to [their] parents" (2 Tim. 3:2). As children are to obey their parents, so their fathers who are Spirit-filled are commanded in Ephesians 6:4, "do not provoke your children to wrath."

Following the relationship of husbands and wives to each other, and of children to their parents, Paul treated the relationship between servants and their masters. In Ephesians 6:5, Spirit-filled servants are to be obedient to their masters, and in verse 9, masters who are walking in the Spirit will treat their servants as they would wish their servants to treat them if their situations were reversed.

We know that since not all people turn to Christ, the world will never be guided in its totality by the principles laid down for those who are Spirit-filled. And we know that since not all believers are or will be Spirit-filled, the churches will not totally function this way either.

However, when Spirit-filled believers obey God, who enables them to live in the power of His Spirit, they are harbingers of the new age, which has dawned but has not yet fully come.

The perfect age awaits the return of the Lord Jesus, when evil will be eliminated forever and believers will be perfectly sanctified and eternally Spirit-filled. Until that time arrives, we can be sure that marital problems, problems with children, and employee and employer difficulties will be commonplace. But amid all of these evils, some of the people of God will manifest the signs of the new age by the way they act and live. This will resound to the glory of Jesus Christ.

4. *Sometimes we hear that when people are filled with the Spirit their problems will lessen or even disappear, but is this what the Scriptures teach?*

Your problems may lessen, or they may change to new problems. But they are not likely to disappear. In Ephesians 6:10, we see that Spirit-filled men and women can be strong in the Lord. They can be spiritual giants among the petty and the defeated. In verse 11, they are said to be warriors who are clad with the whole armor of God. They will not fight against each other. Their enemies are external to them; not flesh and blood, but principalities and powers, the spiritual hosts of wickedness in the heavenly places. But having armor is not enough.

Spirit-filled warriors are to be "praying always" *in the Spirit* (v. 18). It is good to pray; it is better to pray in the Spirit, for when we do this we are praying in the will of God. And when we pray in the will of God, we obtain what we pray for. It will not be prayer offered for selfish purposes. Rather, it will be prayer for the glory of God and the fulfillment of the divine purposes for the universe.

If we were to summarize this glorious privilege and this steady state under the Holy Spirit, we would say, as Paul did, that the "flesh with its passions and desires" has been crucified. Then we are able to live in the Spirit, and whoever has life in the Spirit will also walk by the Spirit (see Gal. 5:24–25).

Spirit-filled believers become people of courage. But they

also become people who are fruitful. When they witness and testify, something happens in the hearts and lives of the people to whom they witness. The Acts of the Apostles records the amazing results that attended the work of Spirit-filled believers. In Acts 2:41, we read that three thousand souls were converted under the preaching of Spirit-filled Peter, who was described by the ecclesiastical leaders as an idiot. In Acts 5:14, "multitudes of both men and women" were added to the Lord. In Acts 6:7, "the number of the disciples multiplied greatly in Jerusalem, and a great many of the priests were obedient to the faith." In Acts 9:35, "all who dwelt at Lydda and Sharon saw him and turned to the Lord." In Acts 14:1, "a great multitude both of the Jews and of the Greeks believed." In Acts 18:8, "many of the Corinthians, hearing, believed and were baptized."

Spirit-filled believers are fruitful indeed, but God does not automatically shield them from persecution and times of testing. Success breeds enemies among those who do not respond to the gospel message. And they express their enmity in powerful threatenings and personal abuse. Persecution attends the ministry of true Spirit-filled followers of the Lamb. In Acts 2:13 the disciples were accused of being drunkards. In Acts 4:21, the Jewish leaders threatened the disciples. In Acts 5:33, they "were furious and took counsel to kill them." In Acts 5:40, when they had "beaten them, they commanded that they should not speak in the name of Jesus." In Acts 7:59, they stoned Stephen to death. In Acts 8:1, "a great persecution arose against the church which was at Jerusalem." In Acts 9:23, "the Jews plotted to kill" Paul. In Acts 13:50, "the Jews . . . raised up persecution against Paul and Barnabas, and expelled them from their region." In Acts 14:5, an "attempt was made by both Gentiles and Jews, with their rulers, to abuse and stone them." In Acts 14:19, "they stoned Paul and dragged him out of the city, supposing him to be dead."

There are many other incidents of this sort. Even though we may not have experienced what Paul and others went through, we can say that in some places around the globe, true Spirit-filled believers experience the same treatment accorded the apostles in the early church. The more Christians live in the power of the Spirit, the more they are looked upon as enemies and regarded with hatred and disdain.

5. *Will the Holy Spirit help one relate better to people who are not filled with the Holy Spirit?*
It depends upon what you mean by "better." More compassion toward the lost, yes. Guaranteed smooth sailing, no.

Christians who have not been filled with the Spirit sometimes are provoked by what they see and do not understand in the Spirit-filled lives of others. The unfilled sometimes are critical and even bitter toward those who do not hesitate to speak about how they were filled with the Spirit. On occasion, those whose experience includes the gift of tongues are prone to press the gift more than the Giver of the gift, and thus alienate the listener. Moreover, some believers resist what they feel to be the armtwisting of the Spirit-filled who are overly insistent in their approach to others to whom they witness. The cause and effect syndrome is beautifully illustrated for us in the life of George Whitefield.

Whitefield was a Spirit-filled evangelist, one of the greatest of them all. At one time in his early life, he considered the possibility of marriage. He gave every appearance of having fallen in love with Elizabeth Delamotte. When writing about it to a friend he said, "I find from Blendon letters that E . . . D . . . is in a seeking state only. Surely that will not do. I would have one that is full of faith and the Holy Ghost." (Arnold A. Dallimore, *George Whitefield* [London: Banner of Truth Trust, 1970], p. 474). Whitefield was full of the Holy Ghost. He knew what this meant, and he wanted a life partner who was also full of the Holy Ghost. Being full of the Spirit, Whitefield believed he was taught by the Spirit, and that the Spirit spoke to his heart about certain matters in ways beyond the understanding of some of his peers. The great hymn writer and minister, Isaac Watts, said of Whitefield,

> I wish that Mr. Whitefield had not risen above any pretences to the ordinary influence of the Holy Spirit, unless he could have given some better evidences of it. He has acknowledged to me in conversation that he knows an impression on his mind to be divine, though he cannot give me any convincing proofs of it [Ibid., p. 343].

The well known Dr. Philip Doddridge said, "I think, what he says and does comes but little short of an assumption of inspiration and infallibility [Ibid., p. 343]." Bishop Butler in a conversation with John Wesley about himself and George Whitefield said:

> I once thought you and Mr. Whitefield well-meaning men; but I cannot think so now. For I have heard more of you; matters of fact, sir. And Mr. Whitefield says in his journal: "There are promises still to be fulfilled in me." Sir, the pretending to extraordinary revelations and gifts of the Holy Ghost is a horrid thing—a very horrid thing! [Ibid., pp. 343–4].

Whitefield provided the opportunity for these criticisms by statements like this: "What Christ tells us by His Spirit in our closets, that let us proclaim upon the housetops. He who sends us will protect us." Whitefield could claim in his journal, "Preached with more power than ever (that was in the morning). . . . Preached with great power in the evening" (Ibid., p. 362).

Whitefield did know when he had power, great power, and more power. He believed the Holy Spirit did reveal to him the knowledge of the divine will, and he held these things as certainties. His critics spoke as they did because they had not seen or experienced anything beyond what they thought to be the ordinary operations of the Holy Spirit. Furthermore, they did not believe there was any activity of the Holy Spirit beyond what they thought to be His ordinary work.

6. *How does the laying on of hands relate to the filling of the Holy Spirit?*

Some Christians think that the incidental apostolic practice of the laying on of hands for receiving the Holy Spirit is important, perhaps even essential, for those who wish to be Spirit-filled. In Acts 8, the Scripture tells of Philip's evangelistic triumph in Samaria. Miracles and signs were manifested. Numbers of men and women, including Simon the sorcerer, believed on Jesus Christ and were baptized. From Paul's letter, it would appear that those true believers were sealed and indwelt by the Spirit. But they had not received the Holy Spirit.

Peter and John came to Samaria. They prayed for those believers and laid their hands upon them. They then received the Holy Spirit. There is no indication that any of them spoke in tongues. There must have been some manifestation that the reception of the Holy Spirit wrought some change in them that was visible to all. For Simon offered Peter and John money so that he might, through the laying on of his hands, be able to replicate what had happened. Simon was severely rebuked by the apostles. But there is more to the story than this.

Philip was one of the seven deacons. For a man to be eligible for the office, he had to be Spirit-filled. So he had knowledge of what it meant to be Spirit-filled. Why didn't Philip pray for the Samaritans to receive the Holy Spirit, and why didn't he lay hands on them? Did the laying on of hands require the services of an apostle? Obviously, the laying on of hands was not limited to the apostles. In Acts 9, Ananias, who was not an apostle, put his hand on Paul, who then recovered his sight and was filled with the Holy Spirit.

Two incidents in the life of Paul throw further light on early practices. In Acts 16, we read that the Philippian jailer and his family were converted and baptized. Nothing is said about Paul laying hands on them subsequent to their baptism, nor is there any mention of tongues. In the second incident in Ephesus (see Acts 19), Paul acted differently. These believers had received John's baptism. Paul then baptized them in the name of the Lord Jesus. Following the baptism, he laid hands on them. The Holy Spirit came on them, and they spoke in tongues. Moreover, they were given the gift of prophecy, which they used immediately. What the specifics of their prophecy were, we are not told.

The Scripture nowhere lays down specific rules about the laying on of hands to receive the Holy Spirit just as there are not *rules* for fasting. It is simply assumed and done. We learn, however, about the practice of the church in the early centuries regarding the laying on of hands from the writings of the church fathers. Eusebius, the early church historian, has supplied some data on this matter. Two acts were performed when Christ was received by unbelievers: they were baptized and received the laying on of hands.

By his time in history, there were some complications connected with water baptism. The first was the notion that water baptism was essential to salvation; some already accepted the idea of baptismal regeneration. The second had to do with the question of sins committed after baptism. It was generally agreed that all sins committed before baptism were forgiven and the consequences remitted. But post-baptismal sins were looked upon as requiring some form of payment on the part of the one committing those sins. Hence, some people post-poned baptism until their deathbed so they could get the maximum personal benefits, since there would be almost no time between baptism and death, and therefore little need for penance and payment for post-baptismal transgressions.

At any rate, a distinction was made that everyone needed to receive the Holy Spirit subsequent to baptism. It came through the laying on of hands by a bishop, even though baptism itself did not require the services of a bishop. It was generally agreed that anyone dying after baptism and before the laying on of hands by a bishop to receive the Holy Spirit was saved. What, then, did the laying on of hands mean? No one can be saved without being sealed and indwelt. Thus the receiving of the Holy Spirit was something beyond sealing and indwelling. But is the receiving of the Holy Spirit, then and now, impossible unless there is the laying on of hands, and must it be by a bishop?

In the New Testament there were times when the Holy Spirit was received without the laying on of hands. However, we should not suppose that there is no role for the church, or that individualism apart from the functioning church is norma-tive. Those who lay hands on believers cannot convey, through their own power, the receiving of the Holy Spirit. But the laying on of hands may well have an effective function in the receiving of the Spirit, so as to make the experience more meaningful, church-centered, and expressive of the commu-nity aspect of the Christian fellowship.

It is important that believers be taught about receiving the Holy Spirit, exhorted to do what is necessary in order to be filled, and given an opportunity to respond to a public invita-tion to receive the Spirit. The hands of elders and deacons and Spirit-filled brothers and sisters can be laid upon those who ask God to fill them as they open their hearts to the coming of the

Holy Spirit into their lives by way of endowment, or spiritual gifts, and enduement, or power for the use of the gifts and the living of a holy life.

7. Is being filled with the Spirit a "second work of grace?"

Christians need to define their terms carefully when asking this question. We can understand the answer to this question better if we look at the term *salvation*.

Anyone who is saved is saved. But theologically, we say we have been saved, we are being saved, and we will be saved. It is past, present, and future. Our salvation has not fully come until we are glorified after death. The Christian hope lies in the future. But the hope itself is based on the sure Word of God.

So also with the doctrine of grace. We are both saved and sanctified by the grace of God. We will inherit eternal life by the grace of God. Nothing that has to do with the Christian life and walk lies outside the boundaries of God's grace. Being filled with the Spirit is, of necessity, also tied to the grace of God.

Is there, then, any real need to talk about a second work of grace when all of the divine work is related to the grace of God, which is no more or less than the unmerited favor of God by which the righteousness of Jesus Christ is imputed to us? Why not, then, talk about the grace of God in relation to the lordship of Christ, the life of holiness, and the Spirit-filled life without using the adjectival numerals—first, second, third and fourth?

The fact is, the Spirit-filled life is more than static; it is dynamic. It is a constant, consistent walk of faith. The Spirit should never be limited to just a first or second work.

8. What can I do to help persuade people to be baptized or filled with the Spirit and to walk in His power?

It was Paul who declared, "my speech and my preaching were not with persuasive words of human wisdom, but in demonstration of the Spirit and of power" (1 Cor. 2:4). He confirmed, with the Old Testament prophet, that things the "Eye has not seen, nor ear heard, Nor have entered into the heart of man . . . God has revealed them to us through His Spirit" (1 Cor. 2:9,10). The Spirit is the teacher, and believers can have the mind of Christ when they have the Spirit in His fullness. Paul knew what he was talking about by personal experience. What he was and what he did was the result of his having been filled with the Spirit.

One of the first differences that having the fullness of the Spirit makes is becoming spiritual and, thus, effective. A second reason for desiring the Spirit's fullness is that we need the Spirit's power. We will be able to do what is otherwise impossible. Samson could never have slain a thousand Philistines with the jawbone of an ass if he had not had the Spirit's power. King David gained a reputation for himself *vis a vis* Saul, who lost the Spirit's power. "Saul hath slain his thousands, And David his ten thousands" (1 Sam. 21:11). David's exploits were due to the power of the Spirit by whom he was overtaken.

A third difference that being filled with the Spirit makes is that the Spirit-filled person is pleasing to God and is becoming what God wants to make him or her. No one can be a man or a woman after God's own heart who is not Spirit-filled. The Spirit-filled have their feet planted on higher ground. Thus they are consciously aware that they are taught by the Spirit, led by the Spirit, and they *know* they have been filled with the Spirit.

Being filled with the Spirit is the mark of an obedient life. It is the will of God for all of His people, without exception, to enjoy this blessing. It is something we are commanded to be. If we are not Spirit-filled, we are either ignorantly or deliberately disobedient. It is true that obedience is attended by the blessing of God. Jesus said that "there is no one who has left house or parents or brothers or wife or children, for the sake of the kingdom of God, who shall not receive many times more in this present time, and in the age to come everlasting life" (Luke 18:29–30). However, if there were no promise of present blessings, only future ones in the kingdom, obedience, even though costly, would be essential. Believers have been redeemed by the precious blood of Christ (see 1 Pet. 1:18–19) that they might be conformed to the image of Christ the redeemer. Our Redeemer faithfully did the will of His Father, "yet He learned obedience by the things which He suffered" (Heb. 5:8).

Another final difference that being filled with the Spirit makes has to do with the judgment yet to come. Paul referred to this aspect of our salvation directly and indirectly. He said, "we shall all stand before the judgment seat of Christ," and "each of us shall give account of himself to God" (Rom. 14:10,12). In another place, Paul wrote, "we must all appear before the judgment seat of Christ, that each one may receive the things done in the body, according to what he has done, whether good or bad" (2 Cor. 5:10). He then added the admonition, "knowing, therefore, the terror of the Lord, we persuade men" (2 Cor. 5:11).

In 1 Corinthians, Paul indirectly spoke of that which has to do with the coming judgment of believers. He said that every believer stands on the solid foundation that is Jesus Christ. All believers are privileged to build a house on this foundation. He spoke of this as human work, and said what we build will be tried by fire. If what we build is made of hay, straw, and stubble, it will be burned up by the fire but the foundation will remain. Thus, "if anyone's work is burned, he will suffer loss; but he himself will be saved, yet so as through fire" (1 Cor. 3:15).

Then Paul laid down the dictum, "Do you not know that you are the temple of God and that the Spirit of God dwells in you? If anyone defiles the temple of God, God will destroy him. For the temple of God is holy, which temple you are" (1 Cor. 3:16–17). When the people of God are not Spirit-filled, the houses they build on the foundation are not made of gold, silver, and precious stones, which will withstand the fire. Being Spirit-filled thus makes a world of difference when we appear at the judgment seat of Christ. Who wants to enter into eternal life empty-handed?

PART III

MARCHING ON

ELEVEN

The Work of the Spirit in the Years Ahead

At no time in the history of the Protestant Reformation could it be said that Western civilization existed in a "post-Christian era" until today. The Renaissance and the Enlightenment thinkers placed human authority over, rather than under, that of the Bible. As a result of that process, secularization has overtaken the Western world. A spirit of materialism is abroad not only in the West but also among all nations under the sun.

The churches that turned the world upside down during the Reformation and sent missionaries to the ends of the earth are faltering. Most of them have moved steadily away from the faith of the apostles. Evangelism and missionary outreach have slackened precipitously. Sunday school enrollments have diminished and church memberships have declined. Whereas, in bygone days, ten thousand evangelists would gather at Winona Lake for summer conferences on evangelism, very few churches have evangelistic meetings today. The number of evangelists has declined to the point where it would be difficult, if not impossible, to gather five hundred of them from America for a conference on evangelism.

Unless the process of secularization is halted and the post-Christian syndrome reversed, we can expect the situation to worsen in the future. It is true, of course, that there are bright spots in this otherwise dismal picture. There are live and vital congregations here and there. Small and concerned renewal movements have sprung up in the major denominations, but the decay and decline of these churches have neither been reversed nor halted to date. Given these circumstances, it is easy for believers to develop a barricade mentality and to evidence little or no hope for improvement. In times like these, some evangelicals suppose we are in the last of the latter days, that Christ is coming soon, and that the worse things get, the more certain we can be that Armageddon is around the corner.

The history of the church affords us with many illustrations of times when Christians thought the end of the age was at hand. Though these believers were well meaning, they were, nonetheless, mistaken. We must keep two things in mind at all costs. The first is that the end of the age may not be at hand. Therefore it is of the utmost importance for Christians to be busily doing the work of evangelization so that all may hear and many may be converted. Second, if we are living in the end times, or are close to that glorious moment when Christ will come again, there is still no reason to suppose that there cannot be a revival quickening, in which multitudes can be saved.

The end times will be characterized by great persecution of believers. Nevertheless, it is said that the blood of the martyrs is the seed of the church. Along with the great growth of wickedness, there could be the great growth of righteousness. Zechariah spoke of the "latter rain" (10:1), which, some think, refers to the end times when the final fulfillment of Joel's prophecy (2:28) will take place. The Spirit was poured out on all flesh at Pentecost according to Acts 2:17. Multitudes were converted and the Christian faith dealt the death blow to the anti-Christian Greek and Roman culture. The same Spirit is to be poured out on all flesh before the second advent of Jesus Christ. Therefore, we can expect great things to happen.

The Spirit at Work Today

No one can deny that there has been an ever-quickening and deepening emphasis on the person and work of the Holy Spirit in recent years. It has been manifested in myriad forms, and the Spirit's power has been at work in unexpected places, and in ways that few have anticipated. Many signs and wonders have also taken place around the globe—signs that have confounded the wise, and brought bewilderment to those who despise such things, or think them to be of demonic origin. It should be apparent to all that revival quickening may be around the corner and that a vast ingathering of souls may be in the offing.

Many Christians are looking and praying for revival in this age of anxiety, turmoil, and fear. What does it take to bring about a real awakening? A. B. Earle, a great Baptist evangelist of the last century, said something that is as true today as it was in his day:

A fire often begins with a little match. . . . The Great Fire in Portland originated with a fire-cracker. So a work of grace often commences with a single Christian—never with the whole church. As soon as one Christian is filled with the Holy Spirit, he goes after others, to lead them to the Savior, or to induce believers to join him in efforts for a revival. . . .

I have observed, for nearly forty years past, that the secret of success in promoting revivals of religion is in having our own hearts filled with the Holy Spirit. . . .

I am often invited to assist pastors and churches in a series of meetings, with the view to gathering in the multitudes, "who are unreached by the ordinary means of grace." Important as it is to reach this class, I have never found any way of doing so, or of reaching the unconverted in the regular congregations, until Christians were filled with the Holy Spirit, and humbled in the dust in agonizing prayer. . . .

Let me, then, again say to all Christians who desire and labor for the conversion of souls: First, be right yourself; spend days and nights, if necessary, in humiliation, fasting and prayer, until the Spirit comes down upon you, and you feel that you have power with God; then you will have power with men in leading them to Christ [*Bringing in the Sheaves* (Boston, 1882), pp. 16–22, *passim*].

What A. B. Earle said, other better known believers have said with equal clarity. A. B. Simpson in his book *Walking in the Spirit* dwells on the necessity for all Christians to be filled with the Holy Spirit. Then they will walk in the Spirit. He wrote about "praying in the Spirit," which is found in Jude 20. Whenever revivals break out or spiritual awakenings take place, they have their origins in the ministries of Spirit-filled believers who also are mighty prayer warriors. Prayer warriors are those who pray in the Holy Spirit. Before stating what praying in the Holy Spirit means, we should note once again that something like this is not common to all Christians. Only *some* believers pray in the Spirit, although all should do this. Matthew Henry, in his commentary, observes,

Our prayers are then most likely to prevail when we *pray in the Holy Ghost*, that is, under his guidance and influence, according to the rule of his word, with faith, fervency, and constant persevering importunity; this is praying in the Holy Ghost, whether it be done by or without a set prescribed form [vol. 6, p. 1116].

A. B. Simpson and Matthew Henry lay before us the truth that when we pray in the Spirit we pray according to the will of God. Since we do not know what to pray for, or even how to pray, when we pray in the Spirit He teaches us these things. When this is true, the things we ask for will come to pass, because they are the will of God. And what is the will of God must come to pass according to the promise of God, as we have stated earlier.

When we have finished praying, we must then get on with the business of witnessing or preaching to lead people to Christ. When we have been filled and have prayed in the Spirit, there is power to make Christ real to the listener. And this power, says A. B. Simpson, leads people to decisions. "It causes them to do something." Mr. Simpson illustrates this in connection with his assertion that "the power of the Spirit always presses them (that is, men to whom we preach the Word of truth) to action, prompt, decisive, positive action." Then comes his magnificent illustration:

> This is the best test of power. It was the test of ancient eloquence; it was the glory of Demosthenes that while under the eloquence of other orators the multitudes hurrahed for the speaker; under his matchless tongue they forgot all about Demosthenes and shouted with one voice, "Let us go and fight Philip."

When the power of the Holy Spirit is at work, men do not praise the preacher. They decide for God and enlist in the battle against Satan himself.

A. J. Gordon agreed with the teaching of A. B. Earle about the power that comes from being filled with the Holy Spirit. He quoted from Andrew Murray:

> . . . the believer may ask and expect what may be termed a baptism of the Spirit. Praying to the Father in accordance to the two prayers in Ephesians, and coming to Jesus in the renewed surrender of faith and obedience, he may receive such an inflow of the Holy Spirit as shall consciously lift him to a different level from the one on which he has hitherto lived [*The Ministry of the Spirit*, p. 66].

Mr. Gordon went on to enlarge on what happens to God's people when they have the fullness of the Spirit and His power. They exhibit holy boldness, they preach powerful sermons, they die the martyr's death with abandonment. In every instance "this infilling marks a decisive and most important crisis in the Christian life, judging from the story of the apostle's conversion [Paul] to which we have just referred" (p. 84).

A. J. Gordon was well aware of the churchly backsliding in his generation. He wrote,

> So at each stage of the church's backsliding a voice is heard from heaven saying: "He that hath an ear, let him hear what the Spirit saith unto the churches." It is the admonition "of him that hath the seven spirits of God," seven times addressed to his church throughout her earthly history, calling her to return from her false guides and misleading teachers, and to listen to the voice of her true Counsellor" [Ibid., p. 133].

C. I. Scofield edited the *Scofield Reference Bible*. He also wrote a number of books. In his book titled *Plain Papers on the Doctrine of the Holy Spirit,* Scofield stressed the necessity for all believers to be filled with the Spirit. He said, "Nor, Biblically, is the filling with the Holy Spirit indispensable only to to ministers of the Word. The filling is indispensable for *any* service" (p. 75). In other words, Scofield was saying that every believer needs the power for service that comes from the Spirit. Moreover, he was careful to distinguish, as we have in this work, the difference between possessing the Spirit and being filled with the Spirit. He wrote,

> But, while it is true that every regenerate believer is indwelt by the Spirit, and by the Spirit baptized into Christ, it is of the very deepest moment to note that the Acts and Epistles discriminate between *possessing* the Spirit, and being *filled* with the Spirit. . . . That all believers are not "filled with the Spirit" when He takes up His abode in them, and baptizes them into Christ, is due to the fact that they have complied with the condition for the receiving of the Spirit, which is simply faith in Christ (John vii.

39; Gal. iii. 2), but have not complied with the conditions for the filling with the Spirit [Ibid., pp. 48–49].

Scofield believed, then, that believers are sealed and indwelt by the Spirit when they become Christians. But they also need to be filled with the Spirit and this filling comes only after the conditions are met—conditions that he described later in his book. The place where he appears to depart from the current charismatic emphasis relates to signs and wonders and tongues as well as gifts of healings and miracles.

In his reference Bible he wrote, "Tongues and the sign gifts are to cease" (p. 1224). The *New Scofield Reference Bible* repeats this statement (p. 1245). However, in both cases, what is not said is very important. Both rightly affirm that "whether there be tongues, they shall cease," but nowhere do the notes say *when* the tongues shall cease. Paul himself does not say when that will happen.

But there is a further problem. When Paul said tongues shall cease, he did not say that other of the sign gifts would cease. He did not say this of gifts of healing and miracles. Why, then, add to tongues the cessation of the gifts of healing and miracles when the Scripture itself does not do so? And why affirm that sign gifts ceased at the end of the apostolic age, when Scripture itself does not explicitly say this will happen?

In the light of this, the overwhelming evidences continue to mount that the Holy Spirit is at work for healing, miracles, tongues, and the like. Should this not cause us to suppose that C. I. Scofield and those who follow this teaching happen to be mistaken in this one aspect of their teaching? But we need not stumble over the sign gifts, which are secondary and which must be understood within the context of the infilling of the Holy Spirit. Scofield and those who agree with him certainly are saying that even though they do not believe that sign gifts are given today, the filling of the Holy Spirit is given, is essential, and is related to revival quickening and to effective Christian witnessing and service.

C. I. Scofield and other dispensationalists generally would have to agree with A. B. Earle, with whom we started, that the secret for promoting revival and for effective evangelistic outreach is being filled with the Spirit. Since we all can assent to this proposition, let us begin at the point of that agreement and work to see every Christian Spirit-filled.

The Spirit *is* at work now, but He never forces any believer to do what that believer does not will to do. The Spirit is willing and waiting to fill any and all who desire to be filled. At no time in the history of the church have all believers been filled with the Holy Spirit, although all have been sealed and indwelt. It is unlikely that all believers will be filled with the Holy Spirit today. Why not? First of all, it is difficult for Christians to appreciate, or to desire keenly, what they have never enjoyed. Describing the joys of ice cream cannot be understood by those who have never tasted it. Second, the average pulpit expositor has not experienced the Spirit's fullness and therefore does not expound the doctrine. Nor does he manifest through his life and ministry the power that his listeners would be anxious to emulate if they could see it in action.

The Need for Preaching about the Spirit

The people in the pews need to be instructed about this great truth of the Spirit's fullness. They need to be told what they must do to obtain the promised blessing. And they must be urged to respond, so that they may receive the gift God is so desirous of imparting. When they know what their inheritance consists of, and when they realize their need to have it, there is the greatest likelihood that they will appropriate it.

Perhaps the supreme need of the clergy is to be able to answer two questions correctly: (1) Have you been regenerated and how do you know it? (2) Have you been filled with the Holy Spirit and how do you know it? When they have answered the second question affirmatively, they can do something for the believers in the pews. If they do not think they can do it themselves, they can bring in others to do it for them. Unless the truth of the Scripture about the Holy Spirit is preached, one way or another, the people in the pews will never know what they should be told. Happily or unhappily, numbers of Christians are learning about the Holy Spirit outside the worship services of their churches, through friends, Bible studies in homes, or by reading books on the subject.

Surely the first and proper place, the God-ordained place, for believers to hear about the Holy Spirit is from the pulpits in the churches where they worship and celebrate the ordinances or sacraments. If they do not get this instruction, the churches are defective. They are not performing their function properly, and this is unfortunate.

The churches would be helped immeasurably if one or two days' meetings on the Holy Spirit were held in various parts of the United States, so that every pastor and his wife, along with concerned laymen and laywomen, would have the opportunity to participate without having to travel far or expend much money that many might not be able to afford.

The National Association of Evangelicals could promote two-day conferences among its constituencies. The Billy Graham Evangelistic Association could promote such conferences, and the Billy Graham Center at Wheaton College would be a logical meeting place in the Middle West. *Christianity Today* could use its pages to promote this emphasis on the Holy Spirit and carry reports of its progress around North America. One would hope that conferences such as the International Conference for Itinerant Evangelists, held in 1983 in Amsterdam, would major on the need for evangelists to be Spirit-filled. The National Religious Broadcasters could emphasize the importance of this matter at their annual meetings in Washington, D.C.

One thing we can be sure about. When the people of God are Spirit-filled there always has been and there always will be a new outbreak of evangelistic and missionary outreach, in which multitudes will come to know Jesus Christ as Savior.

What has been said about national organizations can also be said for the international scene. Agencies like the World Evangelical Fellowship, and all of its related bodies, could influence the entire world and speed the return of Christ.

Building Bridges

We began by discussing the various groups that have contributed to the emergence of the modern charismatic movement. The end product is a broadly diverse movement without a central rallying point or a generally agreed upon theology, agenda, or long-range purposes and programs. There are substantive differences of opinion and a variety of traditions that keep the movement fragmented. The emphases by some on tongues as the first sign of the baptism, and by others on the doctrine of eradication, are not generally shared by people outside those traditions. Bridges designed to transcend those differences must be built. The time may have come for a national conference for those in the holiness and pentecostal traditions and others who stand outside those traditions. The vitalities of the various traditions could be presented, and the advocates of each tradition could get to know those of other traditions face-to-face.

The building of bridges would make understanding possible, lead to support for the commonalities between groups, and bring into being that spiritual awakening all hope will come. The unity of which we speak does not require the surrender of anything considered vital to the various traditions. It would allow for diversity, knowing that behind the differing traditions lie realities that all support and are anxious to see promoted. What is there to keep us from having intimate fellowship, caring concern, and a spirit of loyalty and cooperation with those who see some things differently from their other brothers and sisters?

Many evangelicals, and particularly those in the dispensational tradition, have entertained severe reservations about the charismatic movement. Curiously, some of the larger denominations whose constituencies include those on the left and the right of the theological spectrum have been more open to the charismatic phenomenon.

One of the most conservative of the large denominations is the Southern Baptist Convention. Its Texas State Convention is the largest of all its state conventions. It was in Texas that a charismatic church was voted out of the local association in which it held membership. The action bespeaks the opposition in Southern Baptist ranks to the charismatic movement. Somehow, that sort of attitude toward the charismatic contribution to protestant orthodoxy needs to be reversed. What we need is for evangelicals everywhere to become more charismatic and for charismatics to become more evangelical!

One of the toughest nuts to crack is the theological difficulty attending the rise, prominence, and churchly approval of the charismatic phenomenon among Roman Catholics. Many of them have come to a clear understanding of justification by faith alone and are just as regenerate as any Protestant believer. The difficulty from the Reformation perspective comes to the fore when converted Roman Catholics remain within that church, generally because they wish to witness to other Roman Catholics about their experience in Jesus Christ. We have mentioned the existence of these theological problems earlier. But when we come to consider the work of the Holy

Spirit in the years ahead we must ask, what should the attitude of non-Roman Catholic charismatics be toward Roman Catholic charismatics?

Perhaps the answer to the question will be found in an editorial that appeared in the October 22, 1982, issue of *Christianity Today*. It was written by W. Stanford Reid, a historian who is professor-emeritus from Guelph University in Ontario, Canada. He spoke of the increasingly conciliatory approach of the pope and others in the Roman Catholic church, toward Protestants. Then he asked, "Has the Church of Rome changed from what it was in the 1530s? Have the causes of the Protestant Reformation really been removed? Or is it that Protestants are giving up their basic principles?"

In response to the question, Dr. Reid said,

> Yet an examination of Rome and its official doctrines today reveals that its teachings have changed relatively little since the sixteenth century. In fact it prides itself that its doctrine never changes. What is infallible may develop, but it never changes from wrong to right. And the Roman church has never rejected the doctrines set forth in the Canons of the Council of Trent (1563). These were specifically propounded in opposition to Protestant teaching, anathematizing such doctrines as justification by faith alone and the sole authority of the Scriptures. At the same time they asserted the doctrines of transubstantiation, baptismal regeneration, and justification by faith *and* works. The Roman church repeatedly celebrates Mass according to the historic rites and in accordance with the doctrines of Trent. . . .
>
> All of this may pose no problem for friendly relations. But any evaluation of the present situation will show that on many crucial points Rome has not officially changed since the sixteenth century. Protestants must keep this in focus if they are to remain true to their Bible-centered faith. For their part, Roman Catholics must recognize the dilemma they pose for evangelicals. Quite apart from the personal beliefs of Roman Catholics today, the church still stands officially committed by its creeds to

doctrines evangelicals cannot accept—and some of them lie at the very heart of biblical faith [pp. 12–13].

So long as the Church of Rome and Protestantism retain their respective theologies, there is little hope for genuine, full-hearted, and unrestricted unity and cooperation. Evangelicals, however, should take into account the possibility of change in the Roman Catholic church by the sovereign work of the Holy Spirit. While there is nothing to suggest such change now, every Protestant believer should pray for the Holy Spirit to work a miracle, in which doctrinal change will produce agreement in accord with Reformation principles.

Building bridges is important indeed. But lines and boundaries must be drawn so that Christianity does not become a mishmash of conflicting and antithetical viewpoints. The uniqueness of evangelical orthodoxy supposes there are boundaries that cannot be crossed, boundaries that rule out those who cannot assent to the faith of orthodoxy, and who, until the boundaries of orthodoxy become theirs, must remain separated from each other this side of eternity.

Charismatic Difficulties

The work of the Holy Spirit in the years ahead can be helped or hindered, depending on the curtailment of certain tendencies found within the charismatic communities. One of the areas of tension involves faith healing, which is often based upon a claim to have the gift of healing.

It is not uncommon for healing evangelists to hold mass meetings in which promises of healing are made and few people are actually healed. I have personally attended a number of such meetings and noted that the wheelchair and stretcher cases rarely seem to get the healer's attention, and the victims go away disappointed. Some healers have used colored cards for which money has been paid. The aura of the commercial is dominant. The healer seems to be the one helped the most, and that from a financial perspective. Some of the most important healers have been challenged to produce bona fide cases of healing that can stand up against the scrutiny of medical investigation. They have not done so.

The existence of the fraudulent enterprises should not blind anyone from acknowledging the existence of the real instances where healing has occurred. Whether such healings are a direct result of prayer or the gift of healing should be looked at carefully. An article entitled "Miracles: Not for Today" appeared in the August 1982 issue of *Moody Monthly*. It was written by John Phillips. The author went to the other extreme when he said, "The gifts of healing and miracles are definitely not for today. The age of the sign miracles died out with the writing of the New Testament and with the Jewish nation's final hardening to the Gospel." At the same time the author said that, "Even today, Christendom can see the miraculous being produced by Spiritists and Christian Scientists. In pagan lands, witch doctors and occultists can also produce these kinds of phenomena." Thus, it appears that unbelievers can produce signs and do wonders that are not possible for believers to do. However, the author does say that God "can heal anyone and He does answer prayer." While sensationalism strikes at charismatics, confusion dogs the evangelicals.

When we turn to the Scriptures, we quickly discover that the gifts of miracles and healings appeared sporadically. One can therefore expect that these gifts, if given today, would be rare but not nonexistent. Moreover, if signs and wonders can be produced through demonic agencies, it seems questionable to suppose that God does not use them today—unless, of course, the Scriptures explicitly say that such gifts are not given in this age. But the Scriptures nowhere make such a statement.

The fact is, there have been times when the gifts of healing and miracles have appeared. Some enthusiasts overstate the case, however, when they attribute miracles and healings to the spiritual *gifts* of miracles and healing when they should be labelled "answers to prayer." When Mr. Phillips, in his article, concedes that healing can come through prayer, the question becomes moot. And who will deny that God performs miracles, even today?

In the interests of charity and our common heritage of theological orthodoxy, it would be better if two things were promoted vigorously today. The first is that there are miracles and healings that take place today, but that, in the main, they derive from prayer rather than from individuals with gifts of healing and miracles. Second, those who claim that sign gifts have died out would do well to examine the evidences that seem to contravene their opinion and instead stress the infrequency of the sign gifts, while acknowledging that they do appear here and there from time to time. A mutual spirit of reticence, as to whether what we have seen, and are seeing afresh today, is from prayer or from the gifts of the Spirit, would allow for what is happening. In the final analysis, we should rejoice in what God is doing and leave open the question whether He is doing it from prayer or from the Spirit's special gifts.

Lest there be any doubt about some of the unusual operations of the Holy Spirit right now, reference can be made to incidents connected with the life and ministry of one of my former students, who teaches at the School of World Mission Pasadena, in California. Dr. Peter Wagner is a former missionary to Latin America, an experienced and mature believer whose word is unquestioned and whose testimony to the incidents that follow can be verified by those who were involved in them. Thus, the incidents are not matters of hearsay but come from the lips of the one who was intimately connected with them.

The first incident took place in St. Louis, Missouri, in connection with a meeting of the Executive Committee for the American Festival of Evangelism. The incident preceded the Festival itself, which convened in Kansas City during the summer of 1980. Prior to the meeting of the Executive Committee, Peter Wagner, Ted Engstrom, and Duncan Brown met for breakfast in the Holiday Inn. They were joined by Tom Zimmerman, who is the head of the Assemblies of God. Dr. Zimmerman had been operated on for several blocked arteries prior to the meeting. He was in a critical situation in the hospital. Following the surgery, he was taking blood thinners to prevent the formation of blood clots.

When Dr. Zimmerman sat down for breakfast he was obviously ailing. He had had open-heart surgery. Complications had developed while he was on the operating table, the recovery period had proved difficult, and he had not bounced back as he had hoped. He had then developed phlebitis in his leg. This inflammation of the vein produced a blood clot, which went to his lung area, and he was hospitalized again. He was given the blood thinners and released from the hospital the day before this breakfast meeting.

When he came to the meeting of the Executive Committee and joined these three other men prior to the meeting, he was feeling very badly. All of the brethren were concerned for him, since this was the first time they had seen him since his open-heart surgery. They were alarmed at his apparent decline.

Dr. Zimmerman told them about his surgery and described the details of his most recent hospital visit. While this was going on something happened to Peter Wagner. He felt a personal anointing come upon him in a way he had never experienced before. He was impelled to pray for Tom Zimmerman there in the booth of the restaurant with waitresses and patrons walking back and forth. There was considerable hubbub, as he asked the others to join him in prayer. He placed his hand on the head of Tom Zimmerman, and the others put their hands on him too. Peter began to pray.

Peter Wagner had been a missionary many years in Latin America, and he had come into contact with many sick people. He had prayed for them, but nobody was healed. Some got worse. He concluded, years before this incident, that he did not have the gift of healing, and he had virtually stopped praying for sick people. But here he was, convinced that he should pray for Tom Zimmerman.

As Peter prayed and the others joined him, something happened. At this moment the warmth of anointing he had felt in his own body, flowed through his arm and onto the head of Dr. Zimmerman. There arose in his heart the deep conviction that Dr. Zimmerman was healed. He told him so. But there was no immediate indication of anything happening.

Several times during the meeting of the Executive Committee, of which Dr. Zimmerman was the chairman, he expressed hopes for the Festival and his participation in it, if he was well enough to do so. Peter Wagner rebuked him publicly and reaffirmed the fact that God had healed him. As Tom Zimmerman chaired the meeting, it was clear that he was not his usual self. The meeting ended and the committee members went home. It was not then apparent that anything remarkable had happened to Tom's physical condition.

The following week, Peter Wagner called Tom Zimmerman's office to talk with him. His secretary answered the phone and said he was in a meeting with other Presbyters of the denomination. Peter asked her how Tom was feeling. She told him that Dr. Zimmerman had come into the office feeling better than he had felt at any time since his open-heart surgery. And he had stopped passing blood the afternoon before Peter's call.

Since then, on at least three occasions, Peter Wagner has

heard Tom Zimmerman tell how that prayer time was the turning point in his recovery from the open-heart operation. He has functioned normally since then, and there has been no more passing of blood in the almost three years since the incident took place.

Peter Wagner has his own healing story to tell as well. He was afflicted with migraine headaches and high blood pressure. Once, for seventy days and nights, he endured a sustained migraine attack. Since 1977, he was on medicine for hypertension, taking three different medications every day. He was prayed for on several occasions. The first time nothing happened. The second time he noticed some improvement. Then he went to a worship service at the Vineyard Christian Fellowship Church of Yorba Linda in California. The pastor, John Wimber, has taught a class at the School of World Mission. He has had an interest, and much experience, in healing.

When Peter Wagner attended Pastor Wimber's church, a call for healing was issued. A member of the congregation had a "word of knowledge," during which time he said there was someone in the meeting who suffered from severe migraine headaches caused by hypertension. The pastor asked if such a person was in the audience. Wagner stood and was then surrounded and prayed for by a small group from the church who minister to those in need of healing. Wagner stated that since the time he was prayed for, his migraine headaches have disappeared, apart from an occasional headache such as most people suffer. But his hypertension remained.

Pastor Wimber was teaching the class at the School of World Mission, having directly to do with healing, miracles, and the like. He said he wanted to demonstrate what he did and how he did it, and he asked if there was anyone in the classroom who was willing to be a guinea pig. Peter Wagner went forward. John Wimber had him sit on a high stool. Then he asked him what he wanted healing for. Wagner told him how he had attended his church and how he had been ministered to for the migraine headaches. He told the class members that he had been freed from the migraines, but he asked, "What about the high blood pressure that I still have?" Wimber replied that maybe God wanted to heal him of that too.

When John Wimber began to pray, Wagner said, "My whole body began relaxing in an incredible way," until he was semiconscious. Wagner could hear everything that was going on. Wimber was telling the class exactly what was happening, "just like a sports announcer on a telecast," Wagner said. Then Wimber said that he had a word from the Lord that healing was beginning and the process would last all night. Wagner was helped off the stool. When he went home, he took his blood pressure and it was the highest it had ever been. The major problem was the elevation of the diastolic pressure. This was the case, even though he was on full medication and had been for some time. The next morning when he took his blood pressure, it was the lowest since he had been on medication.

Pastor Wimber had specifically told him that if he was on medication, only the physician who prescribed the medication should take him off it. Wagner had an appointment to see his physician two weeks after the healing event. He told the physician, who was not a Christian, that he thought he had been healed. The physician said it sounded to him like hypnotism, and he said he had seen some strange things as a result of hypnotism.

When he examined Dr. Wagner, he took him off one of the three medications Wagner had been taking. He told him to return in three months' time. Wagner did so. The physician took him off the second medication and told him to return in four months. When he came back at the end of the four months, the physician took him off the last medication. Wagner is now free of his hypertension and has no headaches. He was healed by the power of God through prayer.

The physician told Wagner that the prayer session with Wimber was evidently the turning point in his hypertension. Whether this healing came about because Pastor Wimber has the gift of healing, or through prayer, without the gift of healing or the gift of faith, is something that cannot be verified. But he was healed, through whatever means, by the power of God.

John Wimber, whose church grew from zero to three thousand in five years, has been teaching a class at the School of World Mission under the title, "MC510: Signs, Wonders, and Church Growth." There have been healings of a notable nature in this class, and some have been "slain in the Spirit." It is this latter manifestation that seems to arouse the greatest adverse reactions among so many Christians. John Wesley recorded an interesting statement in his journal about what happened at a revival meeting in Huntingdonshire in May of 1759, a meeting conducted by the Rev. J. Beveridge, under whose preaching adults and children fell under the power of the Spirit. "They shrieked, swooned, babbled senselessly, cried out in praise of God." In the summer of 1801, a North Carolina Presbyterian congregation saw Spirit manifestations. "Physical manifestations and speaking in tongues made it like the day of Pentecost and none were careless or indifferent." Surely if such things could happen in a staid Presbyterian church, they can happen almost anywhere!

The story of the labors of John Wimber, the class experiences at the School of Mission, and other interesting material appeared in the October, 1982, issue of *Christian Life* magazine. The facts cannot be contraverted and must be looked at in the light of biblical revelation about such matters.

Hindering the Holy Spirit

We have been talking about the glorious work of the Holy Spirit in the lives of God's people. It should be apparent to all that I accept as a fact that some of God's people are filled or baptized with the Spirit, and that nomenclature is purely a secondary matter that should not keep us from appropriating what lies behind differing terms for the same experience. It is also a fact that God, through his Spirit, does perform miracles and healings. Speaking in tongues does happen and is a bona fide gift of the Spirit. There are a few people of God here and there who receive the gifts of healing or miracles. These gifts have not ceased. They are still there even though they occur with less frequency than some people suppose. But the gifts of the Spirit and the filling of the Holy Spirit carry with them built-in dangers, hazards, and snares. These possibilities must be considered.

God Almighty is a jealous God. He will not share His glory with anyone else. The Holy Spirit, the third person of the Trinity, shares that jealousy. God's glory is threatened when the gifts of the Spirit and the fullness of the Spirit that comes to men and women are not appropriately used and acknowledged as His gifts. It is easy for the Spirit-filled to become proud of the fact that they are Spirit-filled. And the filling is lost in the wreckage of pride, which so often is unconsciously present in the lives of some of the people of God. The gifts of the Spirit are subject to misuse and abuse. It is easy for someone to whom a precious gift has been given to lose sight of the unchanging fact that the continued possession and use of the gift is utterly and completely contingent upon the presence and power of the Holy Spirit.

We can see the diminishing of the Spirit's glory among some of those who have been blessed by the fullness and the gifts of the Spirit. The tongues speaker thinks he or she is above those who do not speak in tongues. He or she thinks there is something special that makes him or her worthy of this gift. He or she fails to give glory to the Spirit who is the Giver. Those who have the gift of faith, by which wonderful answers to prayer have come, are tempted to think there is something worthy in themselves, and they begin to use that gift autonomously so that the jealousy of the Spirit is aroused because the divine glory is being attacked.

Who has not run into some dear brother or sister who stresses the life of holiness and sincerely believes that eradication is a reality so that sin is not possible. He or she boasts of not having sinned for twenty years. It would be better for these believers to seal their lips and show by their conduct the holiness they possess, than to spread this claim abroad by their own spoken word. Many an evangelist has fallen by the wayside because he presumed to think that the gift of an evangelist, which was given to him by the Holy Spirit, was his in his own right. When he diminished the power of the Holy Spirit, the Giver, he lost the gift, because the glory of the Giver had been sacrificed on the altar of human pride.

The Spirit *is* at work today. Some miraculous and encouraging things are taking place. The divine power is being manifested in ways that astonish us. But the Spirit works as He pleases and, not always in ways and manners we think He should. He often takes the despised and rejected of the world and does wonderful things in and through them. We could be standing on the edge of a great spiritual awakening in America and around the world. But that awakening will not occur until the Holy Spirit can work among those whose eyes look only for His glory and who are willing to give credit to the Spirit for every happening.

The world has yet to see what the Spirit can do through those who are wholly yielded to Him. He is looking for people who are willing to be humble. For even humility is the gift of the Holy Spirit, whereas pride results in the loss of the Spirit's power. The greatest danger facing those who come under the tutelage of the Holy Spirit for fullness, gifts, and power lies in the temptation to put themselves ahead of the Spirit, instead of behind the Spirit, where they are hidden and sheltered from public view.

Instead of running away from what the Spirit is doing, or closing their eyes to what should be thankfully acknowledged and received by every believer, God's people need to identify themselves with what is going on and join the action. Christians are not called to sit on the sidelines or simply cheer from the bleachers. For the work of the Holy Spirit in the latter days is, of course, not yet completed.

The presence of the Holy Spirit is something that should be emblazoned on a thousand banners, held in the hands of tens of thousands of warriors for Christ, as they march to war against the powers of darkness and rescue millions of benighted heathen who are blinded by the prince of the power of the air. For this is their slogan, their marching order:

> 'Not by might nor by power,
>   but by My Spirit,'
> says the LORD of hosts
> (Zech. 4:6).

Bibliography

Arthur, William. *The Tongue of Fire* (New York: Harper, 1857).

Augsburger, Myron. *Quench Not the Spirit* (Scottsdale, Penn.: Herald Press, 1962).

Berkhof, Hendrikus. *The Doctrine of the Holy Spirit* (Richmond: John Knox, 1964).

Bliss, George R. *Commentary on the Gospel of Luke* (Philadelphia: American Baptist Publication Society, 1882).

Bright, Bill. *The Holy Spirit, The Key to Supernatural Living* (San Bernadino: Here's Life Publishers, 1980).

Carter, Charles Webb. *The Person and Ministry of the Holy Spirit, A Wesleyan Perspective* (Grand Rapids: Baker Book House, 1974).

Chafer, Lewis Sperry. *He That Is Spiritual* (Philadelphia: Sunday School Times Company, 1922).

Christenson, Larry. *A Message to the Charismatic Movement* (Minneapolis: Dimension Books, Bethany Fellowship, 1972).

Clark, Dougan. *The Offices of the Holy Spirit* (Philadelphia: National Publishing Association for the Promotion of Holiness, 1879).

Dallimore, Arnold A. *George Whitefield*, vol. 1 (London: Banner of Truth Trust, 1970).

Dixon, Amzi Clarence, ed., *The Person and Ministry of the Holy Spirit* (Baltimore: Wharton, Barron, 1890).

Ervin, Howard M. *These Are Not Drunken as Ye Suppose* (Plainfield, N.J.: Logos International, 1968).

Gillquist, Peter E. *Let's Quit Fighting About the Holy Spirit* (Grand Rapids: Zondervan, 1974).

Goforth, Jonathan. *By My Spirit* (Minneapolis: Bethany Fellowship, 1942, 1964).

Goodwin, John. *Pleroma to Pneumaticon; or, A Being Filled With the Spirit* (Edinburgh: Nichol, 1867).

Gordon, Adoniram Judson. *Quiet Talks on Power* (Chicago: Revell, 1903).

Gordon, Adoniram Judson. *The Ministry of The Spirit* (Philadelphia: American Baptist Publication Society, 1894).

Graham, William Franklin. *The Holy Spirit* (Waco, Tex.: Word, 1978).

Hackett, Horatio. *A Commentary on the Acts of the Apostles* (Philadelphia: American Baptist Publication Society, 1882).

Hills, Aaron Merritt. *Holiness and Power for the Church and the Ministry* (Cincinnati, Ohio: Revivalist Office, 1897).

Horn, Neville. *A Spirit-Controlled Life: or How to Be Filled With the Holy Spirit* (Lincoln, Neb.: Back to the Bible Publishers, 1962).

Howard, David M. *By the Power of the Holy Spirit* (Downers Grove, Ill.: InterVarsity, 1973).

Joy, Donald Marvin. *The Holy Spirit and You* (Kansas City: Beacon Hill, 1978).

MacNeil, John. *The Spirit-Filled Life* (New York: Revell, 1895).

Mahan, Asa. *The Baptism of the Holy Ghost* (New York: W. C. Palmer, Jr., 1870).

McConkey, James Henry. *The Three-Fold Secret of the Holy Spirit* (Pittsburgh: Silver Publishing Society, 1897).

Moody, Dwight Lyman. *Secret Power, or, The Secret and Success in Christian Life and Work* (Chicago: Moody Colportage Association, 1881).

Murray, Andrew. *The Full Blessing of Pentecost; The One Thing Needful* (New York: Revell, 1908).

Nuttell, Geoffrey Fillingham. *The Holy Spirit in Puritan Faith and Experience* (Oxford: B. Blackwell, 1946).

Pache, René. *The Person and Work of the Holy Spirit* (London: Marshall, Morgan and Scott, 1956).

Scofield, Cyrus I. *Plain Papers on the Doctrine of the Holy Spirit* (Westwood, N.J.: Revell, 1899, 1966).

Simpson, Albert Benjamin. *The Holy Spirit,* 2 vols. (New York: The Christian Alliance Publishing Company, 1895, 1896).

Simpson, Albert Benjamin. *Walking in the Holy Spirit* (Harrisonburg, Penn.: Christian Publications, reprint, 1960).

Smith, Charles Edward. *The Baptism in Fire; The Privilege and Hope of the Church in All Ages* (Boston: Lothrop, c. 1883).

Smith, Oswald J. *The Spirit-Filled Life* (New York: The Christian Alliance Publishing Company, 1926).

Spurgeon, Charles Haddon. *Twelve Sermons on the Holy Spirit* (Grand Rapids: Baker Book House, 1974).

Thoburn, James Mills. *Church of Pentecost* (London: Kelly, 1899).

Thomas, William Henry Griffith. *The Holy Spirit of God* (Chicago: The Bible Institute Colportage Association, 1913).

Torrey, Reuben Archer. *The Baptism with the Holy Spirit.* (New York: Revell, 1895).

Torrey, Reuben Archer. *The Holy Spirit* (New York: Revell, 1927).

Torrey, Reuben Archer. *The Person and Work of the Holy Spirit as Revealed in The Scriptures and Personal Experience* (Grand Rapids: Zondervan, 1968).

Unger, Merrill F. *The Baptism and Gifts of the Holy Spirit* (Chicago: Moody, 1974).

Unger, Merrill F. *The Baptizing Work of the Holy Spirit* (Wheaton, Ill.: Van Kampen, 1953).

Walvoord, John F. *The Holy Spirit at Work Today.* (Chicago: Moody, 1973).